# About Wolters Kluwer Law & Business

Wolters Kluwer Law & Business is a leading provider of research information and workflow solutions in key specialty areas. The strengths of the individual brands of Aspen Publishers, CCH, Kluwer Law International and Loislaw are aligned within Wolters Kluwer Law & Business to provide comprehensive, in-depth solutions and expert-authored content for the legal, professional and education markets.

**CCH** was founded in 1913 and has served more than four generations of business professionals and their clients. The CCH products in the Wolters Kluwer Law & Business group are highly regarded electronic and print resources for legal, securities, antitrust and trade regulation, government contracting, banking, pensions, payroll, employment and labor, and healthcare reimbursement and compliance professionals.

**Aspen Publishers** is a leading information provider for attorneys, business professionals and law students. Written by preeminent authorities, Aspen products offer analytical and practical information in a range of specialty practice areas from securities law and intellectual property to mergers and acquisitions and pension/benefits. Aspen's trusted legal education resources provide professors and students with high-quality, up-to-date and effective resources for successful instruction and study in all areas of the law.

**Kluwer Law International** supplies the global business community with comprehensive English-language international legal information. Legal practitioners, corporate counsel and business executives around the world rely on the Kluwer Law International journals, loose-leafs, books and electronic products for authoritative information in many areas of international legal practice.

**Loislaw** is a premier provider of digitized legal content to small law firm practitioners of various specializations. Loislaw provides attorneys with the ability to quickly and efficiently find the necessary legal information they need, when and where they need it, by facilitating access to primary law as well as state-specific law, records, forms and treatises.

Wolters Kluwer Law & Business, a unit of Wolters Kluwer, is headquartered in New York and Riverwoods, Illinois. Wolters Kluwer is a leading multinational publisher and information services company.

ASPEN PUBLISHERS

# FOR THE FEDERAL RULES OF EVIDENCE

*With Summaries of the*
*Official Advisory Comments*

## Jack S. Ezon, Esq.
## Jeffrey S. Dweck, Esq.

Wolters Kluwer
Law & Business

AUSTIN   BOSTON   CHICAGO   NEW YORK   THE NETHERLANDS

Aspen Publishers
Attn: Permissions Department
76 Ninth Avenue, 7th Floor
New York, NY 10011-5201

To contact Customer Care, e-mail customer.care@aspenpublishers.com,
call 1-800-234-1660, fax 1-800-901-9075, or mail correspondence to:

Aspen Publishers
Attn: Order Department
PO Box 990
Frederick, MD 21705

Printed in the United States of America.

2 3 4 5 6 7 8 9 0

ISBN 978-0-7355-7016-0

**Library of Congress Cataloging-in-Publication Data**

Ezon, Jack S.
  E-Z rules for the federal rules of evidence: with summaries of the official
advisory comments / Jack S. Ezon, Jeffrey S. Dweck.
     p. cm.
  ISBN 978-0-7355-7016-0
   1.  Evidence (Law)–United States–Outlines, syllabi, etc.  I. Dweck,
Jeffrey S. II. United States. Federal Rules of Evidence. III. Title.

  KF8935.Z9E96 2007
  347.73′6–dc22                                        2007022959

Cover illustration: Lael Henderson/Images.com

NOTE: E-Z Rules is not a substitute for the actual text of the official Federal Rules of Evidence and
should not be quoted or cited to. E-Z Rules is meant to be used as a quick reference and guide to
understanding the Federal Rules and cannot completely replace them. In addition, the "Overview"
for each section of the Federal Rules is not meant to be a comprehensive teaching tool, as it does not
consider case law. It is merely meant to provide the general scheme and remind the reader of certain
key points of the Federal Rules of Evidence.

# IMPORTANT NOTE

All rules follow the format of the Federal Rules of Evidence. Where the actual subsection letter or number of the rule is used, it is enclosed between parentheses "( )." All other numbers and letters are produced by E-Z Rules and, therefore, should not be cited to when discussing a rule. These numbers and letters and other E-Z Rules "bullets" have been added in addition to the official subsections found in the actual code in order to make the substance more comprehensive.

For example, in Rule 104 there are five sections, referred to in E-Z Rules as (a) - (e). These are actual sections used in the Federal Rules of Evidence and may be called, for example, "subsection (a)." Under Rule 104(a), however, there are items labeled "1.", "a.", and so forth. Since these are not enclosed in parentheses, they are not the letters or numbers used by the Federal Rules.

# USING E-Z RULES FOR THE FEDERAL RULES OF EVIDENCE

*Why E-Z Rules?*

Welcome to **E-Z Rules**: A new way of presenting rules and laws, designed to put the "ease" into legalese!

**E-Z Rules** translates the confusing statutory language of the Federal Rules into plain and simple English. **E-Z Rules** give you quick access to the important information you need, without the unnecessary strain of dissecting long, monotonous, statutory texts. And remember, **E-Z Rules** does this *without excluding any key points of the actual rule or statute*!

*How Is It Organized?*

**E-Z Rules** is easy to use. It has been carefully tailored to meet the needs of both the law student and today's active law firm.

The **E-Z Rules for the Federal Rules of Evidence** begins with the *Roadmap to the Federal Rules of Evidence* to the key topics of (1) the admissibility of relevant evidence, (2) the competency of the person giving evidence, and (3) authentication. With its Overview, Relevant Rules, and actual Federal Rules of Evidence in **E-Z Rules** format, the *Roadmap* will help you quickly grasp the concepts of the featured key topics.

Following the *Roadmap* are the actual Federal Rules of Evidence (with Committee Notes) — again, in **E-Z Rules** format.

*What Is the E-Z Rules Format?*

- **E-Z Rules** is laid out so that the entire substance of a rule or statute can be grasped at a single glance.
- Rules are boldly titled for quick spotting.
- Key words and phrases are emphasized with either bold, italic, or underline. All defined terms are enclosed in quotation marks so as to alert the reader that the term has a definition provided by the Rules. This not only helps in making the Rules easier to understand, but has been proved to help the user focus on pivotal words or phrases that may otherwise go unnoticed. In addition, certain words have been abbreviated in order to facilitate quick referencing and easier reading.
- All rules follow the format of the Federal Rules of Evidence. Where the actual subsection of the rule is used, it is enclosed between parentheses "( )." All other numbers and letters are produced by E-Z Rules and, therefore, should not be cited to when discussing a rule.
- **E-Z Rules** numbering, lettering, and "bullets" have been added in addition to the official subsections found in the actual code in order to make the substance more comprehensive.

Where the actual subsection letter or number of the rule is used, it is enclosed between parentheses. These are actual sections used in the Federal Rules and may be called, for example, "subsection (a)."

---

**Rule 104. Preliminary Questions**

(a) **Questions of admissibility generally**
1. <u>Answering preliminary questions</u>:
    a. The following preliminary questions are determined by the <u>judge</u>:
        i. The qualification of a person to be a witness
        ii. The existence of a privilege
        iii. The admissibility of evidence
    b. This is subject to subdivision (b).
2. <u>Applicability of the FRE</u>:
    a. The judge is not bound by the rules of evidence in answering these questions
    b. <u>Exception</u>: Questions regarding **privilege**

(b) **Relevancy conditioned on fact**
   *If evidence is only relevant if some factual condition is fulfilled,* the judge will admit such evidence upon/subject to the introduction of supporting evidence that the condition was fulfilled.

(c) **Hearing of jury**
1. <u>Hearings on the admissibility of confessions</u> are always done without the jury present.
2. <u>Hearings on other preliminary matters</u> are so done when:
    a. The interests of justice require
    or b. The accused is a witness <u>and</u> so requests

(d) **Testimony by accused**
   An accused <u>cannot</u> be cross examined on other issues of a case when testifying on a preliminary matter.

(e) **Weight and credibility**
   This rule does not limit the right of a party to introduce to the jury evidence relevant to <u>*weight*</u> or <u>*credibility*</u>.

---

All other numbers and letters, not enclosed in parentheses, are produced by E-Z Rules. They are not the letters or numbers used by the Federal Rules and, therefore, should not be cited to when discussing a rule.

For example, in Rule 104 there are five sections, referred to in **E-Z Rules** as (a) - (e). These are actual sections used in the Federal Rules and may be called, for example, "subsection (a)." Under Rule 104(a), however, there are items labeled "1.", "a.", and so forth. Since these are not enclosed in parentheses, they are not the letters used by the Federal Rules.

*Note:* **E-Z Rules** is not a substitute for the actual text of the Federal Rules and should not be quoted or cited to. *E-Z Rules* is meant to be used as a quick reference and guide to understanding the Federal Rules of Evidence and cannot completely replace it. In addition, the Overview for each section of the *Roadmap to the Federal Rules* is not meant to be a comprehensive teaching tool. It is merely meant to remind you of certain key points.

# SUMMARY OF CONTENTS

# Part One

# ROADMAP
## TO THE
# FEDERAL RULES
# OF EVIDENCE

The E-Rules Roadmap to the Federal Rules of Evidence is designed to put everything you need for a given topic at your fingertips. It is organized by key topic (admissibility of relevant evidence, competency of person giving evidence, and authentication) and provides complete coverage in a format designed to guide you easily through the material.

Each topic begins with an Overview. In the Overview, terms are defined and salient points are highlighted. Following the Overview are (1) a list of the rules applicable to the topic and (2) the actual rule in E-Z style, that is, in language that makes the rule easy to understand.

The Roadmap will help you analyze problems. By using it as a checklist, you can breakdown a problem and "attack" it in a comprehensive and organized fashion and in accordance with the Rules.

Studying the Roadmap will help you grasp the concepts behind the Federal Rules of Evidence and gain an overall picture of the relevant law.

Let the Roadmap guide you to a solution!

# CONTENTS

# ADMISSIBILITY OF RELEVANT EVIDENCE

## WHEN EVIDENCE IS RELEVANT:

### ⬥ OVERVIEW

General rule: Only "relevant evidence" can be admitted (Rule 402).

Definition: **"Relevant evidence"** is evidence that makes a fact more or less likely to be true than it would be without the evidence (Rule 401).

Relevant evidence may be excluded for unfair prejudice, confusion, or waste of time (See Rule 403 for more detail).

Relevant Rules: 401, 402, 403

## Rule 401. Definition of "Relevant Evidence"

**"Relevant evidence"** is evidence that makes a key fact either more or less likely to be true than it would have been without the evidence.

*See Part II for summary of Official Advisory Comments.*

## Rule 402. Relevant Evidence Generally Admissible; Irrelevant Evidence Inadmissible

a. All **relevant evidence** is <u>admissible,</u> *unless* otherwise provided by:
　　1. The U.S. Constitution.
　or　2. An act of Congress.
　or　3. The FRE.
　or　4. Other rules prescribed by the U.S. Supreme Court pursuant to statutory authority.

b. Evidence that is **not relevant** is <u>inadmissible</u>.

*See Part II for summary of Official Advisory Comments.*

## Rule 403. Exclusion of Relevant Evidence on Grounds of Prejudice, Confusion, or Waste of Time

Relevant evidence may be excluded if its value is substantially outweighed by *either*:

　　1. <u>The danger of</u>:
　　　　a. Unfair prejudice.
　　or　b. Confusion of the issues.
　　or　c. Misleading the jury.

or  2. <u>Considerations of</u>:
      a. Undue delay.
   or  b. Waste of time.
   or  c. Needless presentation of cumulative evidence.

*See Part II for summary of Official Advisory Comments.*

# TYPES OF EVIDENCE

## ⬍ OVERVIEW

There are two general types of evidence:

- Direct: Evidence relating directly to the question of fact (example: Al testifies that he saw Abe kill Lee).
- Circumstantial: Evidence that may indirectly shed light on a question of fact (example: Al testifies that Abe is very temperamental, hates Lee, and can get very violent at times).

There are special rules dealing with certain types of circumstantial evidence (without weighing the prejudice on a case-by-case basis); these include the following:

1. Evidence describing a person's **character** (Rule 404).
2. Evidence of a person's **habits** (Rule 406).
3. Evidence regarding **subsequent remedial measures** of a person (Rule 407).
4. Whether a person has offered to **compromise** or compromised (Rule 408).
5. Whether a person offers to **pay medical expenses** (Rule 409).
6. Evidence regarding a person's **pleas** and related statements (Rule 410).
7. Whether a person has **liability insurance** (Rule 411).
8. Evidence regarding a person's **sexual behavior** (Rules 412-415).

## *Character Evidence*

"Character evidence" is evidence of a person's character or character traits.

**Generally inadmissible.** Normally, character evidence is inadmissible if it is used to show that person acted in a certain way (example: Moe sues Alan for breach of contract and gets Harold to testify that Alan is known to be a liar. Harold's testimony would normally not be admissible to prove that Alan lied to Moe in this particular transaction).

The rules address two different types of character evidence:
1. Character of the accused or alleged victim in a criminal case:
   - *Generally:* Character evidence would be admissible if the accused offered character evidence about himself, or if the accused offered evidence, and the prosecution wanted to rebut this evidence with contrary character evidence (Rule 404(a)). The prosecution may also offer evidence of a character trait where the accused offers the character trait of the alleged victim.
   - *Homicide case:* If the accused initially brings character evidence about the alleged victim in a homicide case, the prosecution may bring up character evidence (of the victim's peacefulness) to prove that the victim was not the aggressor.
2. Character evidence involving other acts, crimes, or wrongs.
   - This type of evidence is inadmissible to show that the accused acted in a certain way, but is admissible for other purposes (this conforms with the general rule of character evidence). Note that in criminal cases, there is a notice requirement (Rule 404(b)).

Acceptable methods of proving character (Rule 405).
- **Reputation or opinion evidence:** Normally, admissible character evidence may be proved only by reputation or opinion evidence (example: Dan accuses Shirley of fraud. Max may introduce evidence that Shirley has a reputation of defrauding her customers to prove that there is no mistake or accident).
- **Specific instances of conduct:** If the character/character trait is an essential element of a charge, claim, or defense, evidence of specific instances of conduct may be used as proof (example: Shirley is being charged with first-degree murder. Max may introduce evidence that she had done something malicious, because malice is an "essential element" of first-degree murder).

**Relevant Rules: 404, 405**

# Rule 404. Character Evidence Not Admissible to Prove Conduct; Exceptions; Other Crimes

(a) **Character evidence generally.**
1. "Character evidence" is evidence of a person's character or character trait.
2. <u>Admissibility</u>:
    a. Character evidence is <u>not admissible</u> to prove that a person acted in keeping with that character.
    b. **Exceptions** (The following character evidence may be admitted):
        (1) **Character of accused (in a criminal case)**, if:
            a. The evidence is <u>offered by the accused</u> and is pertinent.

            or b. The evidence is <u>offered by the prosecution to rebut</u> character evidence offered by the accused.

            or c. The evidence is offered by the prosecution to show the character trait of the accused, <u>where the accused offers the character trait of the alleged victim</u> (under Rule 404(a)(2)), and the evidence is admitted.
        (2) **Character of the alleged victim (in a criminal case and subject to Rule 412 (sex offense cases)**[*]**)**, if:
            a. The evidence is <u>offered by the accused</u> and is pertinent.

            or b. The evidence is <u>offered by the prosecution to rebut</u> character evidence offered by the accused.

            or c. The evidence is offered in a <u>homicide case and is</u>:
                i. Offered by the prosecution.

                and ii. Offered to show the peacefulness of the alleged victim of the homicide.

                and iii. Used to rebut evidence that the alleged victim was the aggressor.
        (3) Character of the witness (See Rules 607, 608, and 609).

(b) **Admissibility of evidence of other crimes, wrongs, or acts.**
1. Evidence of a person's other crimes, wrongs, or acts is <u>not</u> admissible to prove that the person acted *in keeping with that character*.

---

[*]In a criminal case involving sexual misconduct, the admissibility of evidence of the victim's sexual behavior/predisposition is governed by Rule 412, which is more stringent.

2. <u>Exceptions</u>:
    a. Such evidence may be admissible for other purposes, such as proof of:
        1. Motive.
        2. Opportunity.
        3. Intent.
        4. Preparation.
        5. Plan.
        6. Knowledge.
        7. Identity.
        8. Absence of mistake or accident.
    b. <u>Requirement</u> (in a criminal case): Upon request of the accused, the prosecution must provide *reasonable notice* of the general nature of the evidence, *either:*
        i. <u>Before</u> trial.
    or  ii. <u>During</u> trial, if the court excuses pretrial notice on good cause shown.

*See Part II for summary of Official Advisory Comments.*

# Rule 405. Methods of Proving Character

**(a) Reputation or opinion.**
    1. In cases where character evidence is <u>admissible</u>, proof may be made by:
        a. Testimony as to reputation.
    or  b. Testimony in the form of an opinion.
    2. *Specific instances of conduct* may be explored as proof on cross-examination.

**(b) Specific instances of conduct.**
    1. *Specific instances of conduct* may also be used as proof where a person's character/character trait is an <u>essential element</u> of a charge, claim, or defense.

*See Part II for summary of Official Advisory Comments.*

## *Habits and Routine Practice*

### ⬦ OVERVIEW

Evidence regarding a person's habit or an organization's routine practice is admissible to prove conduct on a particular occasion.

Business practices are usually enough to prove that an organization acted in accordance with those practices on a particular occasion.

Relevant Rule: 406

# Rule 406. Habit; Routine Practice

a. <u>Evidence admissible</u>:
    1. A person's habit.
or 2. The routine practice of an organization.

b. <u>Relevance</u>: The evidence is relevant to prove that certain conduct was in keeping with that habit or routine.

c. The evidence is admissible <u>regardless</u> of:
    1. Whether the evidence has been corroborated.
or 2. The presence of eyewitnesses.

*See Part II for summary of Official Advisory Comments.*

## Subsequent Remedial Measures

**OVERVIEW**

Evidence of a measure that a person takes after an event (that would have made the event less likely to occur had it been taken beforehand) is admissible only to prove:
- Ownership.
- Control.
- Feasibility of precautionary measures.
- Impeachment.

(Example: Carl may prove that he owns Blackacre by showing that he paid taxes and maintained Blackacre after the dispute arose.)

It is inadmissible to prove:
- Negligence.
- Culpable conduct.

(Example: Ralph may not prove that Charles was negligent merely by the fact that after Ralph fell on Charles's sidewalk, Charles had it repaired.)

**Relevant Rule: 407**

## Rule 407. Subsequent Remedial Measures
(Effective December 1, 1997)

*This rule was amended to include product liability actions in the exclusionary principle. It was also amended to clarify that the rule applies only to remedial measures made after the occurrence that caused the damages.*

a. A **"subsequent remedial measure"** is:
    1. A measure that is taken after injury or harm caused by an event.
  and 2. A measure that would have made the injury or harm less likely to occur had it been taken earlier.

b. Evidence of **subsequent remedial measures** taken is:
    1. **Inadmissible** to prove:
        a. Negligence.
    or  b. Culpable conduct.
    or  c. A defect in a product.
    or  d. A defect in a product's design.
    or  e. A need for a warning or instruction.
  but 2. **Admissible** for other purposes, like proving:
        a. Ownership.
    or  b. Control.
    or  c. Feasibility of precautionary measures (if disputed).
    or  d. Impeachment.

*See Part II for summary of Official Advisory Comments.*

## ◆ OVERVIEW

Evidence of a settlement or settlement negotiation is inadmissible to prove:
- Liability of a claim.
- Invalidity of a claim or its amount.

It is admissible to show:
- Bias or prejudice of a witness.
- An absence of a contention of undue delay.
- Obstruction of a criminal investigation/prosecution.

**Relevant Rule: 408**

## Rule 408. Compromise and Offers to Compromise

1. This rule applies to evidence of:
    - (a)(1) Giving or receiving (or offering or promising to give or receive) valuable consideration in a compromise/attempt to compromise a claim.
    - or (a)(2) <u>Conduct</u> at compromise negotiations (regarding the claim) or a <u>statement</u> made in compromise negotiations (regarding the claim).

*Admissible or Inadmissible?*

a. **Inadmissible:**
    1. If used to prove <u>liability</u> for or <u>invalidity</u> of a disputed claim or its amount.
    - or 2. If used to impeach a prior inconsistent statement (or contradiction).

b. **Admissible** for other purposes, like:
    - a. Proving bias of a witness.
    - b. Negating a contention of undue delay.
    - c. Proving an effort to obstruct a criminal investigation or prosecution.

*See Part II for summary of Official Advisory Comments.*

## Offers to Pay for Medical Expenses

**OVERVIEW**

Offers to pay medical expenses are inadmissible to prove liability and admissible for any other relevant purpose.

Relevant Rule: 409

## Rule 409. Payment of Medical and Similar Expenses

Evidence of an offer or promise to pay medical, hospital, or other expenses, or actually paying such expenses, that arose as a result of an injury is <u>inadmissible</u> to prove liability for the injury.

*See Part II for summary of Official Advisory Comments.*

## *Pleas, Discussions, and Related Statements*

**◆ OVERVIEW**

Evidence of a plea or statements connected with a plea in a <u>proceeding for perjury</u> are admissible against a criminal defendant, if the statement was made:
- Under oath.
- On the record.
- In front of counsel.

Such evidence is also admissible if another statement made in the plea discussions was introduced in the proceedings, and it is only fair if this statement is considered together with it.

<u>The following is inadmissible:</u>
- Guilty plea that was later withdrawn.
- *Nolo contendere* plea.
- Statement regarding one of these.

**Relevant Rule: 410**

# Rule 410. Inadmissibility of Pleas, Plea Discussions, and Related Statements

a. <u>Scope</u>: This rule applies to both civil and criminal proceedings.

b. Except as otherwise provided, the following is <u>inadmissible</u> against a defendant who either made a plea or participated in plea discussions:
    (1) Evidence that a guilty plea was later withdrawn.
    (2) Evidence of a *nolo contendere* plea.
    (3) Any statement made in the course of the proceeding under (Federal Rule of Criminal Procedure 11 or comparable state rule) regarding (1) or (2).
    (4) Evidence of <u>plea statements</u>:
        a. Any statement made in the course of plea discussions with a prosecutor that either:
            i. Did not result in a guilty plea.
       or  ii. Resulted in a guilty plea that was later withdrawn.
        b. <u>Exceptions</u>: Plea statements are <u>admissible</u> if either:
            i. Another statement made in the plea discussions has been introduced (and it is only fair if this statement is considered together with it).
       or  ii. In a <u>criminal proceeding for perjury or false statement</u>, where:
               1. The defendant was under oath.
         and 2. The statement was on the record.
         and 3. The statement was made in front of counsel.

*See Part II for summary of Official Advisory Comments.*

## *Liability Insurance*

**OVERVIEW ⬍**

Evidence that a person has insurance is admissible:
- To show agency, ownership, or control.
- To show bias or prejudice.

It is inadmissible to show negligence or other wrongful act.

**Relevant Rule: 411**

# Rule 411. Liability Insurance

Evidence concerning whether or not someone is insured for liability is:

    a. **Inadmissible** to prove negligence or another wrongful act.

    b. **Admissible** for other purposes, like:

        i. Proof of agency, ownership, or control.
        ii. Proof of bias or prejudice of a witness.

*See Part II for summary of Official Advisory Comments.*

*Sexual Behavior*
*a) Rules on Sexual Behavior*

---

## ▲ OVERVIEW

Changes to Rule 412 in 1995:
- Evidence concerning victim's past sexual behavior and sexual predisposition is generally inadmissible.
- The 1995 Rule 412 distinguishes between criminal and civil cases when determining admissibility.
  - For **criminal cases**, the rule is mostly the same except that the new rule has provided a third circumstance for admitting evidence. Evidence of specific instances may be admitted to show past sexual behavior with the accused when offered by the prosecution (not only offered by the accused to prove consent) (Need 412(c) motion).
  - In **civil cases**, the new rule provides for the admissibility of:
    - Sexual predisposition — if the value of the evidence outweighs any danger or prejudice to any party (Need 412(c) motion).
    - Reputation — only if the alleged victim placed it in controversy (Need 412(c) motion).

Added Rules 413, 414, and 415:
- Evidence that the defendant committed similar crimes of sexual assault and child molestation is admissible:
  - In a **criminal case** in which the defendant is accused of that crime.
  - In **civil cases** in which a claim relies on a party's alleged commission of conduct that constitutes an offense of sexual assault or child molestation.

Relevant Rules: 412, 413, 414, 415

---

# Rule 412. Sex Offense Cases; Relevance of Victim's Past Behavior or Alleged Sexual Predisposition

*Rule 412 as* <u>amended</u> *by the Violent Crime Control Act, 1994.*

(a) **Evidence generally inadmissible**: The following is <u>not admissible</u> in any civil or criminal proceeding involving alleged sexual misconduct (see exceptions in (b) and (c)):

    (1) Evidence offered to prove that any alleged victim engaged in *other* sexual behavior.

    (2) Evidence offered to prove any alleged victim's "sexual predisposition."

(b) **Exceptions**

    (1) <u>Criminal case</u>: The following is admissible in a <u>criminal case</u> (if otherwise admissible):

(A) Evidence of specific instances of sexual behavior by the alleged victim <u>and</u> that is offered to prove that someone other than the accused was the source of semen, injury, or other physical evidence.

(B) Evidence of specific instances of sexual behavior by the alleged victim (with respect to the person accused) <u>and</u> that is offered by:

    1. The accused to prove consent.

or 2. The prosecution.

(C) Evidence that if excluded would violate the defendant's constitutional rights.

(2) <u>Civil case</u>: The following is admissible in a <u>civil case</u>:

    a. Evidence offered to prove **sexual behavior/predisposition** of any alleged victim is admissible if:

        1. Otherwise admissible under the FRE.

and 2. Its probative value *substantially outweighs* the danger of harm to any victim and of unfair prejudice to any party.

    b. Evidence of an alleged victim's **reputation** *only if* it has been placed in controversy by the alleged victim.

(c) **Procedure to determine admissibility.**

(1) <u>Requirements of the proponent</u>: Someone who wishes to offer evidence under one of the 412(b) exceptions must:

    (A) **File a motion:**

        1. In writing.

and 2. At least <u>14 days</u> before trial (unless the court, for good cause, requires a different time or allows during trial).

and 3. Specifically describing the evidence.

and 4. Stating the purpose for which it is offered.

and (B) **Serve the motion** on all parties and notify the alleged victim (or the alleged victim's representative or guardian when appropriate).

(2) <u>Requirements of the court</u>:

    a. The court must conduct a hearing in camera and give the alleged victim and parties a right to be heard <u>before trial</u>.

    b. The court must seal the motion, related papers, and the record of the hearing (it may order otherwise).

*See Part II for summary of Official Advisory Comments.*

# Rule 413. Evidence of Similar Crimes in Sexual Assault Cases

*Rule 413 as <u>added</u> by the Violent Crime Control Act, 1994.*

(a) **Admissibility of evidence of similar crimes.**

1. <u>Type of evidence admissible</u>: Evidence that the defendant committed another offense of sexual assault (the evidence is admissible, and may be considered on any relevant matter).

2. <u>When admissible</u>: In a criminal case in which the defendant is accused of an offense of sexual assault.

(b) **Requirements for the government when it intends to offer evidence under this rule**.

    1. <u>Requirement</u>: The attorney for the government must disclose the evidence to the defendant, including statements of witnesses or a summary of any testimony that is expected to be offered.

    2. <u>Time limit</u>:

        a. At least <u>15 days</u> before the scheduled date of trial.

    or  b. At such later time as the court may allow for *good cause*.

(c) This rule shall not be construed to limit the admission or consideration of evidence under any other rule.

(d) **"Offense of sexual assault."** For purposes of this rule and Rule 415, "offense of sexual assault" means a crime under federal law or the law of a state (as defined in 18 U.S.C. §513) that involves:

    (1) Any conduct proscribed by 18 U.S.C. Chapter 109A.

    or  (2) Contact, without consent, between any part of the defendant's body or an object and the genitals or anus of another person.

    or  (3) Contact, without consent, between the genitals or anus of the defendant and any part of another person's body.

    or  (4) Deriving sexual pleasure or gratification from the infliction of death, bodily injury, or physical pain on another person.

    or  (5) An attempt or conspiracy to engage in conduct described in paragraphs (1)-(4).

# Rule 414. Evidence of Similar Crimes in Child Molestation Cases

*Rule 414 as <u>added</u> by the Violent Crime Control Act, 1994.*

(a) **Admissibility of evidence of similar crimes.**

    1. <u>Type of evidence admissible</u>: Evidence that the defendant committed another offense of child molestation (the evidence is admissible, and may be considered on any relevant matter).

    2. <u>When admissible</u>: In a criminal case in which the defendant is accused of an offense of child molestation.

(b) **Requirements for the government when it intends to offer evidence under this rule**.

    1. <u>Requirement</u>: The attorney for the government must disclose the evidence to the defendant, including statements of witnesses or a summary of any testimony that is expected to be offered.

    2. <u>Time limit</u>:

        a. At least <u>15 days</u> before the scheduled date of trial.

    or  b. At such later time as the court may allow for *good cause*.

(c) This rule shall not be construed to limit the admission or consideration of evidence under any other rule.

(d) **Definitions**: For purposes of this rule and Rule 415, **"child"** means a person below the age of 14, and **"offense of child molestation"** means a crime under federal law or the law of a state (as defined in 18 U.S.C. § 513) that involves:

(1) Any conduct proscribed by 18 U.S.C. Chapter 109A that was committed in relation to a child.

or (2) Any conduct proscribed by 18 U.S.C. Chapter 110.

or (3) Contact between any part of the defendant's body or an object and the genitals or anus of a child.

or (4) Contact between the genitals or anus of the defendant and any part of the body of a child.

or (5) Deriving sexual pleasure or gratification from the infliction of death, bodily injury, or physical pain on a child.

or (6) An attempt or conspiracy to engage in conduct described in paragraphs (1)-(5).

## Rule 415. Evidence of Similar Acts in Civil Cases Concerning Sexual Assault or Child Molestation

*Rule 415 as <u>added</u> by the Violent Crime Control Act, 1994.*

(a) **Admissibility of evidence of similar crimes in civil cases**.

1. <u>Type of evidence admissible</u>: Evidence of a party's commission of another offense of sexual assault or child molestation (the evidence is admissible, and may be considered on any relevant matter).

2. <u>When admissible</u>:

a. In a civil case.

and b. In which a claim for damages (or other relief) relies on a party's alleged commission of conduct.

and c. That conduct constitutes an offense of sexual assault or child molestation.

(b) **Requirements for a party who intends to offer evidence under this rule**.

1. <u>Requirement</u>: The party must disclose the evidence to the defendant, *including*:

a. Statements of witnesses

or b. A summary of any testimony that is expected to be offered.

2. <u>Time limit</u>: Disclosure must be made:

a. At least <u>15 days</u> before the scheduled date of trial.

or b. At such later time as the court may allow for *good cause*.

(c) This rule shall not be construed to limit the admission or consideration of evidence under any other rule.

# HEARSAY

## OVERVIEW

Definition:
- Basically, hearsay is a statement made outside of court.
- The rules define hearsay more specifically as "a statement, other than one made by the declarant while testifying at the trial or hearing, offered in evidence to prove the truth of the matter asserted."
- The rules specifically provide that certain statements are not hearsay:
  - Prior statements by witnesses, if the statement:
    - Is inconsistent with the testimony.
    - Is consistent with the testimony and offered to dispute a charge that the person making the statement lied.
    - Identifies a person.
  - Admissions by party-opponents, if the statement was made or adopted by the party or by an agent of the party.

**Relevant Rules: 801, 802**

## Rule 801. Definitions

(a) **"Statement"** includes:
> (1) An oral or written assertion.
> or (2) Conduct (nonverbal) of a person, if that person intended it to be an assertion.

(b) **"Declarant."** A person who makes a statement.

(c) **"Hearsay."**
> 1. A statement offered in evidence to prove that what the statement asserts is true.
> 2. Made by the declarant while not testifying.

(d) **Statements which are not hearsay.**
> (1) **Prior statement by witness:** A prior statement of a witness is not hearsay if:
>> i. The declarant testifies and is subject to cross-examination on the statement.
>> and ii. The statement is either:
>>> (A) Inconsistent with the testimony and was given under oath (at a trial, hearing, other proceeding, or deposition).

or (B) Consistent with the testimony <u>and</u> is offered to dispute a charge (express or implied) that the declarant
      1. Lied.
or  2. Was subject to improper influence.
or  3. Had an improper motive.
or (C) A statement that identifies a person who was seen (or heard).

### (2) **Admission by party-opponent.**

1. A statement that is offered against a party is <u>not</u> hearsay if:
    - (A) The statement is the **party's own statement** (as an individual or as a representative).
    - or (B) The party seems to have **adopted or believed** the statement to be true.
    - or (C) The person making the statement was **authorized** by the party to speak.
    - or (D) The statement was:
        1. Made by an **agent** or **servant**.
        - and 2. Made <u>during the existence</u> of the relationship.
        - and 3. Concerning an issue <u>within the scope</u> of the relationship.
    - or (E) The statement was made by a **co-conspirator** during and in advancement of the conspiracy.

2. The <u>contents</u> of the statement will be considered, but that is <u>not</u> enough in itself to establish any of the following:
    - a. The <u>declarant's authority</u> under (C).
    - b. The <u>agency or employment relationship</u> (and its scope) under (D).
    - c. The <u>existence of a conspiracy</u> and the declarant's participation with the party against whom the statement is offered under (E).

*See Part II for summary of Official Advisory Comments.*


## Rule 802. Hearsay Rule

a. **HEARSAY IS <u>INADMISSIBLE</u>.**

b. <u>Exceptions</u>: Hearsay is <u>admissible</u> where provided for by:
    1. The FRE.
or 2. Other rules prescribed by the U.S. Supreme Court pursuant to statutory authority.

*See Part II for summary of Official Advisory Comments.*

## ⬍ OVERVIEW

Rules 803, 804, and 805 provide exceptions to the hearsay rule. Rule 803 gives exceptions that do not depend on the availability of the declarant, whereas Rule 804 exceptions are conditioned on the declarant's unavailability. Rule 805 gives the exception for "hearsay within hearsay."

**Relevant Rule: 803**

## Rule 803. Hearsay Exceptions; Availability of Declarant Immaterial

**THE HEARSAY RULE <u>DOES NOT</u> APPLY TO THE FOLLOWING (EVEN THOUGH THE DECLARANT IS AVAILABLE AS A WITNESS):**

(1) **Present sense impression.**
    This is a statement:
        a. Describing or explaining an event/condition.
  and b. Made **while** or **immediately after** the declarant was experiencing the event/condition.

(2) **Excited utterance.**
    This is a statement:
        a. About a *startling* event/condition.
  and b. Made while the declarant was under the stress of excitement caused by the event/condition.

(3) **Then existing mental, emotional, or physical condition.**
    a. These are statements of the declarant's then existing (at time statement made):
        1. State of mind.
        2. Emotion.
        3. Sensation.
        4. Physical condition.
        5. <u>Examples</u>: Intent, plan, motive, design, mental feeling, pain, bodily health.
    b. This does not include statements of memory (to prove the fact remembered) or belief (to prove the fact believed) unless the statement is about the <u>declarant's will</u>.

(4) **Statements for purposes of medical diagnosis or treatment.**
    These are statements:
        a. Made for purposes of medical diagnosis or treatment.

and b. Describing any of the following (as long as they are reasonably related to the diagnosis or treatment):

    1. Medical history.

or  2. Past or present symptoms, pain, or sensations.

or  3. The general character of the cause of them.

## (5) Recorded recollection.

a. This is a memorandum or record that:

    1. Concerns an issue that the witness had knowledge about but can no longer remember enough to testify fully and accurately.

and 2. Was made or recorded when the issue was fresh in the mind of the witness.

and 3. Correctly represents the witness's knowledge.

b. If admitted, the memorandum or record may be read into evidence but may not be submitted as an exhibit (unless offered by an adverse party).

## (6) Records of regularly conducted activity.

a. <u>Records are not hearsay if</u>:

    1. <u>They are one of the following items</u>:

        A. Memoranda.

    or  B. Reports.

    or  C. Records.

    or  D. Data compilations (in any form).

and 2. <u>They record</u>:

        A. Acts.

    or  B. Events.

    or  C. Conditions.

    or  D. Opinions.

    or  E. Diagnoses.

and 3. <u>They are recorded</u>:

        A. By a person with knowledge.

    and B. From information communicated by a person with knowledge.

and 4. The item was kept in the course of a regularly conducted business activity.

and 5. <u>When recorded</u>: Made at or near the time of the act or event.

and 6. It is regular practice of that business activity to make such records, etc.

and 7. All of the above (1-6) must be shown by the <u>custodian</u> of the records or some <u>other qualified witness</u>, *unless* there is a lack of trustworthiness (as shown by the source of information or the method or circumstances of preparation), in which case the evidence would be <u>inadmissible</u>.

This can also be shown by a <u>Rule 902(11) certification</u>, a <u>Rule 902(12) certification</u>, or by <u>a statute permitting certification</u> (e.g., 18 U.S.C. § 3505: "Foreign Records in Criminal Cases").\*

   b. **"Business"** means profit/nonprofit business, institution, association, profession, occupation, or calling of any kind.

(7) **Absence of entry in records kept in accordance with the provisions of paragraph (6).**

   a. <u>This includes</u>: Evidence that shows that a matter never occurred/existed because:

      1. It is normally included in a paragraph (6) record or report.

  and 2. It is not included.

   b. <u>Exception</u>: If the sources of information or other circumstances indicate lack of trustworthiness, then this type of evidence is <u>inadmissible</u>.

(8) **Public records and reports.**

   a. <u>Public records and reports are not hearsay if</u>:

      1. They are one of the following items:

         A. Records.

      or  B. Reports.

      or  C. Statements.

      or  D. Data compilations (in any form).

  and 2. <u>They are recorded by</u>:

         A. Public offices.

      or  B. Public agencies.

  and 3. <u>They record the following material</u>:

         (A) The office's/agency's <u>activities</u>.

      or  (B) Matters that the office or agency observed and had to report on by duty of law *unless* they are matters observed by police officers/other law enforcement personnel in criminal cases.

      or  (C) <u>Factual findings</u> are admissible in civil cases and against the government in criminal cases if produced by an investigation that was conducted with legal authority.

   b. <u>Exception</u>: If the sources of information or other circumstances are not trustworthy.

(9) **Records of vital statistics.**

   a. <u>Items included</u>: Records/data compilations (in any form) of:

      1. Births.

      2. Fetal deaths.

      3. Deaths.

      4. Marriages.

---

\*This point was amended December 1, 2000, to add ways of satisfying the 803(6) foundation requirements without the expense and inconvenience of time-consuming foundation witnesses.

b. <u>Requirements</u>:
    1. The report was made <u>to a public office</u>.
and 2. The report was made <u>pursuant to requirements of law</u>.

**(10) Absence of public record or entry.**
    a. <u>This includes</u>: Evidence proving the absence of:
        1. Records.
        2. Reports.
        3. Statements.
        4. Data compilation (in any form).
        5. Nonexistence of a matter of which public records are regularly made and preserved.
    b. <u>Requirement</u>: Evidence of the absence may either be:
        1. A Rule 902 certification.
    or 2. Testimony that after a *diligent search* no record, etc., was found.

**(11) Records of religious organizations.**
The hearsay rule does not apply to statements of the following in a <u>regularly kept record</u> of a religious organization:
    a. Births.
    b. Marriages.
    c. Divorces.
    d. Deaths.
    e. Legitimacy.
    f. Ancestry.
    g. Relationship by blood or marriage.
    h. Other similar facts of personal/family history.

**(12) Marriage, baptismal, and similar certificates.**
    a. This includes statements of fact contained in a certificate that the maker:
        1. Performed a marriage.
    or 2. Performed some other ceremony.
    or 3. Administered a sacrament.
    b. These statements must have been made by:
        1. A clergyman.
    or 2. A public official.
    or 3. Another person authorized by a religious organization or by law to perform the act.
    c. **Time of statement**. Statement must have been made *either*:
        1. At the time of the act.
    or 2. At a reasonable time after the act.

**(13) Family records.**
    a. This includes statements concerning personal or family history.
    b. These are statements that are contained in:
        1. Family Bibles.

      2. Genealogies.

      3. Charts.

      4. Engravings on rings.

      5. Inscriptions on family portraits.

      6. Engravings on urns, crypts, or tombstones.

      7. Other similar items.

**(14) Records of documents affecting an interest in property.**

    a. These are records proving:

      1. The **content** of an original document intended to establish or affect a property interest.

  and 2. The **execution** and **delivery** of the original document by each person who the document says executed it.

    b. Requirements:

      1. The record used as evidence must be a record of a public office.

  and 2. An applicable statute must authorize the recording of that kind of document in that office.

**(15) Statements in documents affecting an interest in property.**

    a. This includes statements in paragraph (14) records that are relevant to the purpose of the document.

    b. Exception: When dealings with the property (since the document was made) have been inconsistent with the truth of the statement or the document's substance and intent.

**(16) Statements in ancient documents.**

These are statements in documents that are:

    a. Over 20 years old.

  and b. Authentic (See Rule 901(b)(8)).

**(17) Market reports, commercial publications.**

    a. Items included:

      1. Market quotations.

      2. Tabulations.

      3. Lists.

      4. Directories.

      5. Other published compilations.

    b. Requirement: Items must be generally used and relied upon by:

      1. The public.

  or 2. Persons in particular occupations.

**(18) Learned treatises.**

    a. Items included: Statements in:

      1. Published treatises.

  or 2. Periodicals.

  or 3. Pamphlets.

b. <u>Subject matter of items must be</u>:
1. History.
or 2. Medicine.
or 3. Another Science or Art.
c. <u>Requirements</u>:
1. The statement was:
a. <u>Called to the attention</u> of an expert witness on cross-examination
or b. <u>Relied upon</u> by the expert witness in direct examination
2. The item is a reliable authority as shown by:
a. The testimony of the witness.
or b. Admission of the witness.
or c. Other expert testimony.
or d. Judicial notice.
d. If admitted, these statements <u>may be read</u> into evidence but <u>may not be submitted</u> as an exhibit.

**(19) Reputation concerning personal or family history.**
a. The <u>hearsay rule does not apply to **reputation**</u> concerning a person's:
1. Birth.
2. Adoption.
3. Marriage.
4. Divorce.
5. Death.
6. Legitimacy.
7. Relationship by blood, adoption, or marriage.
8. Ancestry.
9. Similar personal or family history.
b. <u>This includes reputation among</u>:
1. Family members by blood, adoption, or marriage.
or 2. Associates.
or 3. The community.

**(20) Reputation concerning boundaries or general history.**
The hearsay rule does not apply to reputation in a community (arising before the controversy) as to:
1. Boundaries of lands in the community.
2. Customs affecting lands in the community.
3. Events of general history that are important to the community (or state or nation where the community is located).

**(21) Reputation as to character.**
The hearsay rule does not apply to reputation of a person's character among:
1. Associates.
or 2. The community.

(22) **Judgment of previous conviction.**
- a. The hearsay rule does not apply to <u>evidence of judgments</u> used to prove any fact if:
  - 1. Judgment is <u>final</u>.
  - and 2. Judgment was entered *either*:
    - a. After a trial.
    - or b. After a guilty plea (not a *nolo contendere* plea — see Rule 410).
  - and 3. The crime adjudged has a penalty of *either*:
    - a. Death.
    - or b. More than one year in prison.
  - and 4. <u>Requirement</u>: The fact to be proved must be one that was *essential to sustain the judgment*.
- b. This <u>does not include</u> judgments against persons other than the accused that are:
  - 1. Offered by the government as evidence.
  - and 2. Offered in a criminal prosecution.
  - and 3. Offered for purposes other than impeachment.
- c. The pendency of an appeal may be shown but has no effect on admissibility.

(23) **Judgment as to personal, family, or general history, or boundaries.**
- a. The hearsay rule does not apply to judgments used to prove the following matters:
  - 1. Personal, family, or general history.
  - 2. Boundaries.
- b. <u>Requirements</u>:
  - 1. The matter must have been essential to the judgment.
  - and 2. The matter would be provable by evidence of reputation (see Rules 19, 20, 21).

*See Part II for summary of Official Advisory Comments.*

## When Declarant Is Unavailable

**OVERVIEW**

Rule 804 exceptions are conditioned on the declarant's unavailability.
- Grounds for unavailability:
  - The declarant is exempt because the subject matter of his statement is privileged.
  - The declarant refuses to testify.
  - The declarant testifies to a lack of memory.
  - The declarant is unavailable because of death or illness (mental or physical).
- Admissible statements: (The hearsay rule does not apply to the following types of evidence if the declarant is unavailable):
  - Former testimony.
  - Statement made under belief of impending death about cause of injury or illness.
  - Against financial interests or tending to subject declarant to civil/criminal liability.
  - Family history.
  - Other statements that carry a guarantee of trustworthiness.

Relevant Rule: 804

## Rule 804. Hearsay Exceptions; Declarant Unavailable

(a) **Definition of unavailability.**
  - i. A declarant is "unavailable as a witness" where the declarant:
    - (1) Is exempt because the subject matter of his statement is privileged.
    - or (2) Persists in refusing to testify (even after court orders to do so).
    - or (3) Testifies to a lack of memory.
    - or (4) Is dead or suffers a physical or mental sickness.
    - or (5) Is absent <u>and</u> the user of the statement cannot bring the declarant in (or declarant's testimony for 804(b)(2), (3), or (4)) by *reasonable means*.
  - ii. <u>Exception</u>: Where the above is a result of the *user's* wrongdoing intended to prevent a declarant from attending.

(b) **Hearsay exceptions.**
  The hearsay rule does not apply to the following (if the declarant is unavailable as a witness):
    - (1) **Former testimony.**
      - a. <u>When testimony was given *either*</u>:

           1. As a witness at another hearing in the same or a different case.

or   2. In a deposition taken during the same or another case.

  b. <u>Requirement</u>:

      1. The current adverse party had to have a chance and similar motive then (i.e., when the testimony was formerly given) to develop the testimony by direct, cross, or redirect examination.

      2. In civil cases, it suffices that a predecessor in interest to the adverse party now had a chance and motive.

(2) **Statement under belief of impending death**: This statement must be:

  a. <u>Made by</u> declarant who believed that she was about to die.

and b. <u>Concerning</u> the cause or circumstances of the expected death.

and c. In *either*:

      1. A civil action or proceeding.

or   2. A prosecution for homicide.

(3) **Statement against interest.**

  a. <u>Types of statements this refers to</u>:

      1. A statement so far against the declarant's financial interest.

or   2. A statement tending to subject the declarant to civil or criminal liability.

or   3. A statement tending to show that the declarant's claim against another is invalid.

or   4. A statement offered to exonerate the accused by exposing the declarant to criminal liability, <u>only if</u> supporting circumstances show that the statement is <u>trustworthy</u>.

  b. <u>Required standard</u>: *A reasonable person in the same position* would not have made the statement unless he believed it was true.

(4) **Statement of personal or family history.**

  This includes statements:

    (A) Concerning the declarant's:

      1. Birth.

or   2. Adoption.

or   3. Marriage.

or   4. Divorce.

or   5. Legitimacy.

or   6. Ancestry.

or 7. Relationship by blood, adoption, or marriage.

or 8. Other similar facts of personal/family history (even if the declarant had no way to obtain personal knowledge of the matter stated).

or (B) Concerning 1-8 above, or death of another person, if the declarant was:

    1. Related by blood, adoption, or marriage

or 2. Intimately associated with the other's family (i.e., she was likely to have accurate information concerning the issue).

**(5) Other exceptions.**

*This subsection was deleted and moved to Rule 807 (with subsection (24) of Rule 803).*

**(6) Forfeiture by wrongdoing.**

A statement offered against a party, where:

    a. The party was involved in wrongdoing that was intended to make the declarant unavailable as a witness.

and b. The wrongdoing actually did make the declarant unavailable.

*See Part II for summary of Official Advisory Comments.*

*Hearsay within Hearsay*

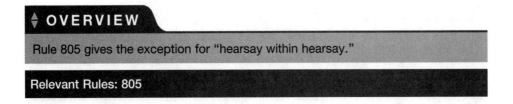

## Rule 805. Hearsay within Hearsay

The hearsay rule does not apply to **"hearsay within hearsay"** if <u>each part</u> of the combined statements satisfies an exception to the hearsay rule (one of the exceptions in Rules 803 or 804).

*See Part II for summary of Official Advisory Comments.*

## *Residual Exception*

**OVERVIEW**

Rule 807 gives additional exceptions.

Relevant Rules: 807

# Rule 807. Residual Exception

Other statements (not covered by 803 or 804) are <u>not</u> excluded by the hearsay rule if the court determines that:

A. The statement is offered as <u>evidence of a material fact</u>.

and B. The statement is the <u>best evidence</u> that the user can obtain through *reasonable efforts*.

and C. Admitting the statement will best serve *the general purpose of these rules* and *the interests of justice*.

and D. The evidence has an equivalent "guarantee of trustworthiness" as the other exceptions in Rules 803 and 804.

and E. The user of the evidence notifies the adverse party in advance (to provide a fair opportunity to prepare) of the:
1. **Intention** to use the statement.
2. **Specifics** of the statement, including the declarant's name and address.

# EVIDENCE DEALING WITH THE CREDIBILITY OF A WITNESS

## ▲ OVERVIEW

Any party may attempt to impeach a witness, or dispute her credibility by introducing evidence about that witness.

The rules address the limitations on the admissibility of certain types of evidence that a party may bring to dispute the witness's credibility.

Types of evidence:

**Evidence of character of witness.**
- Opinion and reputation evidence will be limited to truthfulness (only after truthfulness has been attacked) and untruthfulness of the witness.

**Evidence of conduct of witness.**
- Evidence of a witness's conduct may be proved only by what the witness says, as long as the instances are probative of truthfulness or untruthfulness.
- If the conduct at issue refers to conviction of a crime, then extrinsic evidence (beyond what the witness says) may be used to prove conviction of a crime (as per Rule 609).

**Evidence of conviction of crime.**
- Convictions of crimes involving dishonesty or falsehood are admissible (If the elements of a crime (regardless of punishment) require proof (or admission, in the case of a guilty plea) of an act of dishonesty or a false statement by a witness).
- Evidence of a conviction of a crime is inadmissible if:
  - More than 10 years have passed.
  - Conviction was a juvenile adjudication (unless necessary in a criminal case).
  - The witness has been pardoned and has not committed a crime punishable by more than one year in prison.
- **Religious beliefs or opinions** are not admissible to prove credibility.
- **Extrinsic evidence of prior statements.**
  - Witness must be given a chance to explain/deny the evidence.
  - Opposing party must be given a chance to interrogate the witness on the evidence.

Relevant Rules: 607, 608, 609, 610, 613

## Rule 607. Who May Impeach

Any party (including the party calling the witness) may attack the credibility of a witness.

*See Part II for summary of Official Advisory Comments.*

## Rule 608. Evidence of Character and Conduct of Witness

(a) **Opinion and reputation evidence of character.**

    (1) When dealing with the **character** of the witness, opinion or reputation evidence will be limited to <u>truthfulness</u> or <u>untruthfulness</u>.

    (2) Evidence of <u>truthful character</u> is admissible only after the witness's character of truthfulness has been attacked (by opinion or reputation testimony or otherwise).

(b) **Specific instances of conduct.**

    1. Specific instances of a witness's conduct that are used to support or attack a witness's "character for truthfulness" can be proved only by what the witness says in cross-examination, and not outside evidence.

    2. <u>Requirements</u>:

        a. The "instances" have to be probative of *truthfulness or untruthfulness.*

        b. The <u>cross-examination</u> must concern:

            (1) The witness's character for truthfulness.

      or  (2) The character for truthfulness of another witness as to whom the witness testified.

    3. <u>Exception to 608(b)</u>: Conviction of a crime may be proved by extrinsic evidence (see Rule 609).

    4. The court has discretion whether or not to allow cross-examination.

    5. A witness testifying <u>does not</u> waive the privilege against self-incrimination as to questions that bear <u>only</u> on his character for truthfulness.

*See Part II for summary of Official Advisory Comments.*

## Rule 609. Impeachment by Evidence of Conviction of Crime

(a) **General rule.**

    (1) <u>Admissibility of evidence attacking the truthfulness of a witness</u>:

        a. <u>Witness other than an accused</u>: Evidence that a witness has been convicted of a crime is <u>admissible</u> (subject to Rule 403) *only* if:

       1. The crime is punishable by death.

or  2. The crime is punishable by more than one year in prison.

    b. <u>Accused as witness</u>: Evidence that the accused has been convicted of a crime is <u>admissible</u> if its "probative value outweighs its prejudicial effect to the accused" (court has discretion).

(2) If the elements of a crime (regardless of punishment) require proof (or admission, in the case of a guilty plea) of an act of <u>dishonesty</u> or a <u>false statement</u> by a witness, evidence as to that crime is <u>admissible</u> against any witness.

**(b) Time limit.**

  1. Evidence of a conviction is admissible only until <u>the *later* of</u>:

    a. <u>10 years</u> after the conviction date.

or  b. <u>10 years</u> after the release of the witness from prison (for the conviction in the testimony).

  2. <u>Exception to 10-year time limit</u>: Evidence of a witness's conviction will be admitted after 10 years if:

    a. The court determines *"in the interests of justice"* that "the probative value of the conviction supported by specific facts and circumstances *substantially outweighs* its prejudicial effect."

and b. <u>Notice is given</u>: The party using the evidence gives the adverse party notice of intent to use the evidence:

      1. In advance.

and 2. In writing.

  3. <u>Purpose</u>: To allow the adverse party to contest the use of the evidence.

**(c) Effect of pardon, annulment, or certificate of rehabilitation.**

<u>Evidence of a conviction is inadmissible if</u>:

(1) **Effect of rehabilitation** —

    a. The conviction was the subject of:

      1. A pardon.

or  2. An annulment.

or  3. A certificate of rehabilitation.

or  4. Any other procedure based on the rehabilitation of the convict.

and b. The convict <u>was not</u> convicted of a later crime that was:

      1. Punishable by death.

or  2. Punishable by more than one year in prison.

or (2) **Effect of finding of innocence** — The conviction was the subject of:

    a. A pardon.

or  b. An annulment.

or  c. Any other procedure based on a finding of innocence.

(d) **Juvenile adjudications.**

> Evidence of juvenile adjudications is <u>admissible</u> only if:
> 1. The case is a criminal case.
> and 2. The witness is someone other than the accused.
> and 3. Conviction of the event would be admissible against the credibility of an adult.
> and 4. The court believes that admission is <u>necessary</u> to fairly determine guilt or innocence.

(e) **Pendency of appeal.**

> 1. <u>Effect on admissibility of a conviction</u>: The pendency of an appeal does not render evidence of a conviction inadmissible.
> 2. <u>Admissibility of the pendency itself</u>: Evidence of the pendency of an appeal is admissible.

*See Part II for summary of Official Advisory Comments.*

# Rule 610. Religious Beliefs or Opinions

A witness's beliefs or opinions on <u>religious matters</u> are not admissible to weaken or strengthen the witness's credibility.

*See Part II for summary of Official Advisory Comments.*

# Rule 613. Prior Statements of Witnesses

(a) **Examining witness concerning prior statement.**

> 1. When questioning a witness about a prior statement (written or not), the attorney does not have to show or disclose the contents of that prior statement to the witness.
> 2. On request, the attorney has to show or disclose the contents of the statement to opposing counsel.

(b) **Extrinsic evidence of prior inconsistent statement of witness.**

> 1. Extrinsic evidence of a prior inconsistent statement is admissible only if:
>     a. *Both*:
>         i. The witness is given a chance to explain/deny the evidence.
>         and ii. The opposite party is given a chance to interrogate the witness on the evidence.
>     or b. *The interests of justice otherwise require.*
> 2. This does not apply to 801(d)(2) admissions (admissions of a party-opponent).

*See Part II for summary of Official Advisory Comments.*

# "BEST EVIDENCE RULE" — EVIDENCE PROVING CONTENTS OF WRITINGS

## ♦ OVERVIEW

The original of any writing is required to prove its content.

Duplicates are admissible unless there is a genuine question as to the authenticity of the original or it would be unfair under the circumstances.

Other evidence (example: oral evidence of the contents) may be used under one of the following four circumstances:
• The originals were lost or destroyed.
• The original is not obtainable.
• The opponent has the original.

The writing is not closely related to a controlling issue.

Relevant Rules: 1001, 1002, 1003, 1004

## Rule 1001. Definitions

(1) **"Writings and recordings."**
    a. <u>Writings and recordings consist of</u>:
        1. Letters.
      or 2. Words.
      or 3. Numbers.
      or 4. Their equivalent.
    b. <u>Form</u>:
        1. Handwriting.
        2. Typewriting.
        3. Printing.
        4. Photostatting.
        5. Photographing.
        6. Magnetic impulse.
        7. Mechanical or electronic recording.
        8. Other form of data compilation.

(2) **"Photographs"** include:
    a. Still photographs.
    b. X-ray films.
    c. Video tapes.
    d. Motion pictures.

(3) **"Original."**
    a. <u>Writings and recordings</u>:

      1. A writing or recording itself.

or  2. Any counterpart intended to have the same effect by a person executing or issuing it.

  b. <u>Photographs</u>:

      1. The negative.

or  2. A print from the negative.

  c. <u>Computer-stored data</u>:

      1. Any accurate printout.

or  2. Any other accurate output readable by sight.

(4) **"Duplicate"** is a counterpart produced:

  a. By the same impression as the original.

or  b. From the same matrix as the original.

or  c. By means of photography (including enlargements and miniatures).

or  d. By mechanical or electronic rerecording.

or  e. By chemical reproduction.

or  f. By other equivalent techniques that are accurate.

*See Part II for summary of Official Advisory Comments.*

# Rule 1002. Requirement of Original

The **original** of any writing, recording, or photograph is required to prove its **content**, *unless* provided for by:

    1. Act of Congress.

or  2. The FRE.

*See Part II for summary of Official Advisory Comments.*

# Rule 1003. Admissibility of Duplicates

A **duplicate** is admissible to the same extent as the **original** *unless*:

  (1) There is a *genuine question* as to the authenticity of the original.

or  (2) Under the circumstances it would be unfair to allow the copy instead of the original.

*See Part II for summary of Official Advisory Comments.*

# Rule 1004. Admissibility of Other Evidence of Contents

Other evidence of the content of a writing, recording, or photograph is admissible in place of an original if:

  (1) **The originals were lost or destroyed.** All originals are either lost or have been destroyed, *unless* the proponent lost/destroyed them in bad faith.

(2) **The original is not obtainable:** No original can be obtained by any judicial procedure.

(3) **The original is in possession of an opponent.** An opposing party who has possession of the original does not produce it at a hearing, even after receiving notice that its contents would be a subject of proof at a hearing.

(4) **Collateral matters.** The writing, recording, or photograph is not closely related to a controlling issue.

*See Part II for summary of Official Advisory Comments.*

# COMPETENCY OF PERSON GIVING EVIDENCE

*After determining admissibility of the evidence itself, the Rules consider the person giving the evidence.*

# LAY PERSON

## *Competency of Person Giving Evidence*

**◆ OVERVIEW**

General rule of competency:

Every person is presumed competent to be a witness.

A witness may testify to a matter only if she has personal knowledge of that matter.

Competency of judge as witness:

The trial judge may not testify as a witness.

Competency of juror as witness:

At trial: A juror may not testify before the jury of which he is a member. Inquiry into validity of verdict/indictment:
- A juror may testify as to extraneous prejudicial information and outside influence.
- A juror may not testify as to:
  - Matters or statements made during deliberations.
  - Thoughts or emotions.
  - Mental processes.

**Relevant Rules: 601, 602, 605, 606**

## Rule 601. General Rule of Competency

a. Except as otherwise provided by these rules, <u>every person is competent to be a witness</u>.

b. Where state law applies to a claim or defense, state law shall determine the competency of a witness.

*See Part II for summary of Official Advisory Comments.*

## Rule 602. Lack of Personal Knowledge

a. A witness may testify to a matter only if there is <u>sufficient evidence</u> that the witness has *personal knowledge* of that matter (this evidence may include that witness's testimony).

b. This rule is subject to Rule 703 (optional testimony of an expert witness).

*See Part II for summary of Official Advisory Comments.*

## Rule 605. Competency of Judge as Witness

a. The trial judge may not testify as a witness.

b. <u>Automatic objection</u>: The opponent need not make an objection in order to enforce this (it is "automatic").

*See Part II for summary of Official Advisory Comments.*

## Rule 606. Competency of Juror as Witness

(a) **At the trial.**
    1. A member of the trial jury may not testify as a witness before the jury of which he is a member.
    2. The opponent may object <u>out of the jury's presence</u> if the juror is called to testify.

(b) **Inquiry into validity of verdict or indictment.**
    1. When there is an inquiry into the validity of a <u>verdict</u> or <u>indictment,</u> a juror <u>may not</u> testify as to:
        a. Any matter or statement made <u>during jury deliberations</u>.
    or  b. Anything of that juror's <u>thoughts or emotions</u> that caused the juror to agree/disagree with the verdict or indictment.
    or  c. The juror's <u>mental processes</u> in connection with agreeing/disagreeing with the verdict or indictment.
    2. <u>Exception</u>: A juror may testify as to:
        1. Whether any extraneous prejudicial information was improperly brought to the jury's attention.
    or  2. Whether there was any outside influence on any juror.
    or  3. Whether there was a mistake in entering the verdict onto the verdict form.
    3. This rule also applies to juror affidavits or evidence of jurors' statements (involving the validity of a verdict or indictment).

*See Part II for summary of Official Advisory Comments.*

## *Credibility of Declarant of Hearsay Exceptions*

### ♦ OVERVIEW

A party may call into question the credibility of a declarant who makes an admissible hearsay statement or a statement not considered hearsay (801(d)(2)(C),(D), & (E) statements).

For credibility, the declarant is treated as a witness and may be cross-examined.

The declarant does not have to be given a chance to explain/deny any evidence of his statement or conduct.

**Relevant Rule: 806**

## Rule 806. Attacking and Supporting Credibility of Declarant

a. <u>This rule applies when</u>:
   1. Hearsay statements are admitted into evidence.
   2. Statements defined in Rule 801(d)(2)(C), (D), and (E) are admitted into evidence.

b. The credibility of the declarant may be attacked/supported by any evidence that would be admissible had the declarant testified as a witness.

c. The declarant does not have to be given a chance to <u>deny</u> or <u>explain</u> any evidence of her statement or conduct.

d. If a party against whom a hearsay statement has been admitted calls the declarant as a witness, the party may examine the declarant on the statement as if under cross-examination.

*See Part II for summary of Official Advisory Comments.*

# EXPERTS

**OVERVIEW**

The rules make a distinction between expert witnesses and other types of witnesses.

<u>Definition</u>: An expert is a person who has some special skill, knowledge, experience, training, or education.

<u>When opinion testimony admissible</u>: Unlike lay witnesses, an expert may offer her opinion in many circumstances.

- **Nonultimate issue.** Experts' opinions are generally admissible to provide scientific, technical, or other specialized knowledge so long as the expert has specialized knowledge.
- **Ultimate issue.** Opinion testimony on an "ultimate issue" is admissible unless it is used to show an accused party's criminal state of mind.
- **Underlying facts and data of opinion.**
  - Opinion testimony is admissible even if the expert does not first testify to the underlying facts or data, unless required by the court or perhaps if asked on cross-examination.
  - The opinions can be based on facts that the expert perceives or is informed of at or before the hearing.
  - These facts or data do not have to be admissible as evidence if experts in the field reasonably rely on facts or data of the same type.

Relevant Rules: 702, 703, 704, 705

## Rule 702. Testimony by Experts

a. An expert's **opinion** (or other form of testimony) can be used to provide **scientific, technical,** or **other specialized knowledge,** if it is helpful for *either*:

    1. Understanding the evidence.
    2. Determining a fact in issue.

b. An **"expert"** is someone who is qualified by:

    1. Knowledge.
or  2. Skill.
or  3. Experience.
or  4. Training.
or  5. Education.

c. Reliability:

    The expert testimony will be admissible only if:

        (1) The testimony is based upon sufficient facts or data.

and (2) The testimony is the product of reliable principles and methods.

and (3) The witness has applied the principles and methods reliably to the facts of the case.

*See Part II for summary of Official Advisory Comments.*

## Rule 703. Bases of Opinion Testimony by Experts

a. An expert can base **opinions** and **inferences** on facts/data that:
1. The expert perceives.
2. The expert is informed of at or before the hearing.

b. If experts in the field *reasonably rely* on the same type of facts or data (as in the case) when they form their opinions, the facts or data do not have to be admissible as evidence.

c. Facts or data that are otherwise inadmissible (see b.) may not be disclosed to the jury by the expert or by inference, <u>unless</u> the court determines that the probative value (in helping the jury evaluate the expert's opinion) *substantially outweighs* the prejudicial effect.

*See Part II for summary of Official Advisory Comments.*

## Rule 704. Opinion on Ultimate Issue

(a) Normally, **opinion testimony** is not open to objection just because it *embraces an "ultimate issue"* to be decided by the trier of fact.

(b) <u>Mental state exception</u>: An expert's **opinion testimony** may not be used to show that an accused had a particular mental state or condition that constitutes an element of a crime or a defense. (The trier of fact must determine this on its own.)

*See Part II for summary of Official Advisory Comments.*

## Rule 705. Disclosure of Facts or Data Underlying Expert Opinion

a. An expert witness does not have to testify about the facts or data that underlie her **opinion** or **inference**.

b. <u>Exceptions</u>: The expert <u>must</u> testify about underlying facts if:
1. The Court requires it.
2. The expert is asked to disclose the facts on cross-examination.

*See Part II for summary of Official Advisory Comments.*

# AUTHENTICATION

## CONDITION PRECEDENT TO ADMISSIBILITY

**OVERVIEW ⬍**

Tangible objects will not be admitted into evidence until they are "authenticated" (i.e., proof must be brought that the evidence is "genuine").

Types of tangible objects include writings, records, maps, crime weapons, reports, etc.

Standard of authenticity: The Rules require that the evidence of authentication be *"sufficient to support a finding that the matter in question is what the proponent claims."*

Self-authentication: Certain types of objects are so likely to be what they are that the rules deem them to be "self-authenticated."

Special rules exist for authenticating certain types of documents (See 901(b)).

Relevant Rules: 901, 902, 903

## Rule 901. Requirement of Authentication or Identification

(a) **General provision.**
   1. **Authentication** or **identification** is required as a condition precedent to admissibility.
   2. This requirement is satisfied by "evidence sufficient to support a finding that the matter in question is what its proponent claims."

(b) **Illustrations:** The following are merely examples (not limitations) of **authentication** or **identification**.
   (1) <u>**Testimony of witness with knowledge**</u>: Testimony that a matter is what it is claimed to be is sufficient for authentication.
   (2) <u>**Nonexpert opinion on handwriting**</u>: The opinion may be used to authenticate handwriting so long as it is based upon familiarity not obtained for purposes of the litigation.
   (3) <u>**Comparison by trier or expert witness**</u>: For authentication/ identification, it is sufficient to compare with specimens that have been authenticated.
   (4) <u>**Distinctive characteristics and the like**</u>: The following characteristics may be used so long as they are taken in conjunction with the circumstances:
      a. Appearance.
      b. Contents.
      c. Substance.

d. Internal patterns.

e. Other distinctive characteristics.

(5) **Voice identification can be used if**:

a. <u>Voices that can be identified can be heard *either*</u>:

1. Firsthand.

or  2. Through mechanical or electronic transmission.

or  3. Through mechanical or electronic recording.

and b. The opinion of the voice identification is based on hearing the voice under circumstances connecting it with the alleged speaker.

(6) **Telephone conversations** can be authenticated if:

i. Evidence is provided that a call was made to the number assigned at that time to a particular person/business.

and ii. *Either*:

(A) <u>Person</u>: Circumstances (including self-identification) show that the person who answered was the one called.

or  (B) <u>Business</u>:

1. The call was made to a place of business.

and 2. The conversation related to business that is usually done over the phone.

(7) **Public records or reports** can be authenticated with evidence that a writing is from the public office where such items are recorded or kept.

(8) **Ancient documents or data compilation** can be authenticated with evidence that they are:

(A) In a condition raising no suspicion as to their authenticity.

and (B) In a place where authentic documents are likely to be.

and (C) Over 20 years old.

(9) **Process or system** may be identified with evidence describing the process and showing that it produces an accurate result.

(10) **Methods provided by statute or rule**. Authentication may also be done as provided for by:

a. Act of Congress.

or  b. Other rules prescribed by the U.S. Supreme Court pursuant to statutory authority.

*See Part II for summary of Official Advisory Comments.*

## Rule 902. Self-Authentication

The following do not need outside evidence for authentication:

(1) **Domestic public documents under seal**. If a document has:

a. A seal of:

1. The United States.

or  2. Any state, district, commonwealth, or territory.

or　3. Any insular possession of a state, district, commonwealth, or territory.

or　4. The Panama Canal Zone.

or　5. The Trust Territory of the Pacific Islands.

or　6. Any political subdivision, department, officer, or agency of the above-listed

and　b. A signature purporting to be an attestation or execution.

(2) **Domestic public documents not under seal.** If a document has <u>no seal</u>, but:

1. It purports to have the signature of an officer or employee of an entity listed in (1).

and　2. A public officer who (has a seal and official duties in the district of the officer) certifies under seal that:

a. The signer has the official capacity.

and　b. The signature is genuine.

(3) **Foreign public documents** purporting to be executed and attested by an official may be self-authenticated if they are accompanied by:

i. A certification as to the genuineness of the signature and official position of:

(A) The person executing or attesting to the document.

or　(B) Any foreign official whose certificate of genuineness of signature and official position somehow relates to the execution or attestation.

ii. The certification may be made by:

a. A secretary of an embassy or legation.

or　b. Consul general.

or　c. Consul.

or　d. Vice consul.

or　e. Consular agent of the United States.

or　f. A U.S.-assigned diplomatic or consular official of the foreign country.

iii. If all parties have been given reasonable opportunity to check the authenticity, the court may, *for good cause shown*:

1. Order that they are *presumed authentic* without certification.

or　2. Permit them to be evidenced by an attested summary (even without certification).

(4) **Certified copies of public records.**

a. This includes:

1. Copies of official records or reports (or an entry in a record or report).

2. Copies of documents authorized by law to be recorded or filed (and actually recorded or filed), including data compilations.

b. These must be certified as correct by an authorized person:

1. By certificate complying with 902(1), (2), and (3).

or 2. By complying with an act of Congress.

or 3. By complying with other rules prescribed by the U.S. Supreme Court pursuant to statutory authority.

(5) **Official publications** purporting to be issued by public authority, including:

    a. Books.

    b. Pamphlets.

    c. Other publications.

(6) **Newspapers and periodicals.** Printed materials purporting to be newspapers or periodicals.

(7) **Trade inscriptions and the like**, if:

    a. The trade inscriptions, etc.:

        1. Purport to have been fixed in the course of business.

    and 2. Indicate ownership, control, or origin.

    b. "Trade inscriptions" includes:

        1. Inscriptions.

    and 2. Signs.

    and 3. Tags.

    and 4. Labels.

(8) **Acknowledged documents.** Documents accompanied by an acknowledgment executed:

    1. In a manner provided by law.

    2. By a notary public or other authorized officer.

(9) **Commercial paper and related documents.**
This includes:

    1. Commercial paper.

    and 2. Signatures on commercial paper.

    and 3. Documents relating to commercial paper (to the extent provided by general commercial law).

(10) **Presumptions under Acts of Congress.**
"Any signature, document, or other matter declared by Act of Congress to be presumptively or prima facie genuine or authentic."

(11) **Certified domestic records of regularly conducted activity.**

    a. If a domestic record of regularly conducted activity would be admissible under 803(6) (see Amendment), the original or duplicate of that record would be admissible, so long as it is accompanied by a <u>written declaration</u> (by the custodian or some other qualified witness) certifying the following:

        (A) The record was made at or near the time of the occurrence of the matters set forth by (or from information transmitted by) a person with knowledge of those matters.

    and (B) The record was made in the course of *regularly conducted activity*.

and (C) The record was made by the regularly conducted activity *as a regular practice.*

b. The written declaration is to be made in such a way that complies with any act of Congress or rule prescribed by the Supreme Court (pursuant to statutory authority) (e.g., 28 U.S.C. §1746).

c. A party offering a record into evidence under Rule 902(11) must:

    1. Provide written notice to all adverse parties.

and 2. Make the record and the declaration available for inspection in advance of the offer into evidence (sufficient to provide an adverse party a fair opportunity to challenge the foundation set forth in the declaration).

(12) **Certified foreign records of regularly conducted activity.**

a. If a foreign record of regularly conducted activity would be admissible under 803(6) (see Amendment), the original or duplicate of that record would be admissible, so long as it is accompanied by a <u>written declaration</u> (by the custodian or some other qualified witness) certifying the following:

    (A) The record was made at or near the time of the occurrence of the matters set forth by (or from information transmitted by) a person with knowledge of those matters.

and (B) The record was made in the course of *regularly conducted activity.*

and (C) The record was made by the regularly conducted activity *as a regular practice.*

b. This subsection applies only in <u>civil cases</u>.

c. The declaration must be signed in such a way that if the declaration is false, the maker would be subject to criminal penalty under the laws of the country where the declaration was made.

d. A party offering a record into evidence under Rule 902(11) must:

    1. Provide written notice to all adverse parties.

and 2. Make the record and the declaration available for inspection in advance of the offer into evidence (sufficient to provide an adverse party a fair opportunity to challenge the foundation set forth in the declaration).

*See Part II for summary of Official Advisory Comments.*

## Rule 903. Subscribing Witness' Testimony Unnecessary

A subscribing witness's <u>testimony is not necessary</u> to authenticate a writing, <u>*unless*</u> required by the jurisdictional laws (whose laws govern the writing's validity).

*See Part II for summary of Official Advisory Comments.*

Part Two

# THE
# FEDERAL RULES
# OF EVIDENCE
# IN E-Z RULES FORMAT

# CONTENTS

**ARTICLE I**
# GENERAL PROVISIONS

## Rule 101. Scope

a. <u>The Federal Rules of Evidence apply to cases</u>:
   1. In U.S. courts.
   and 2. Before bankruptcy judges.
   and 3. Before magistrate judges.

b. These rules govern to the extent stated in <u>Rule 1101</u>.

> **Summary of Advisory Committee's Notes on Rule 101**
> Rule 101 specifies in detail the courts, proceedings, questions, and stages of proceedings to which the rules apply in whole or in part.

## Rule 102. Purpose and Construction

a. These rules should be construed to secure:
   1. Fairness in administration.
   and 2. The elimination of expense and delay.
   and 3. The promotion of growth and development of the law of evidence.

b. **The goal of these rules** is that *"truth may be ascertained and proceedings justly determined."*

> **Summary of Advisory Committee's Notes on Rule 102**
> This is similar to Rule 1 of the Federal Rules of Civil Procedure and Rule 2 of the Federal Rules of Criminal Procedure.

## Rule 103. Rulings on Evidence

(a) **Erroneous rulings on evidence.**
   1. For a ruling that either <u>admits</u> or <u>excludes</u> evidence, an error may be found only if:
      i. The ruling affects a <u>substantial right</u> of the party.
      and ii. <u>A party makes *either* an</u>:
         (1) **Objection** — *For a ruling admitting evidence*:
            a. A timely objection or motion to strike must appear on the record.
            and b. Specific grounds (if not already apparent) must also appear on record.
         or (2) **Offer of proof** — *For a ruling excluding evidence*:
            a. Substance of evidence must have been made known to the court by offer.

        or   b. Substance of evidence must have been apparent from questioning.

      2. Once the court makes a definitive ruling on the record (either at or before trial) a party need not renew an objection/offer of proof to preserve its claim of error for appeal.

**(b) Record of offer and ruling.**

      The court may:

        1. Add to the record statements concerning:

           a. The character of the evidence.

        or   b. The form of the evidence.

        or   c. The objection.

        or   d. The ruling.

        2. *"Direct the making of an offer in question and answer form."*

**(c) Hearing of jury.**

        1. Inadmissible evidence must not be suggested to the jury.

        2. <u>Examples of ways of suggesting inadmissible evidence</u>:

           a. Making statements in front of the jury.

           b. Asking questions in front of the jury.

**(d) Plain error.**

      Notice may be taken of <u>plain errors</u> that affect <u>substantial rights</u>, even if not brought to the attention of the court.

---

**Summary of Advisory Committee's Notes on Rule 103**

- Rulings on evidence cannot be assigned error unless (1) a substantial right is affected, and (2) the nature of the error was called to the attention of the judge.
- The objectives here are to alert the judge of the proper course of action and enable opposing counsel to take proper corrective measures. The objection and offer of proof accomplish these objectives.
- This rule has no effect on the law with respect to harmless error.
- The purpose of subdivision (b) is to reproduce for an appellate court as much of what happened in the trial court as possible.
- The second sentence is designed to resolve doubts as to what testimony the witness would have in fact given, and to provide an appellate court with material or a final disposition of the case (in noninjury cases) in the event a ruling that excluded evidence is reversed.
- Subdivision (c) supposes that a ruling that excludes evidence may be pointless if the evidence comes to the attention of the jury.
- Finally, subdivision (d), which is the same as the wording in the Criminal Procedure rule, will be more likely applied to the admission of evidence than to the exclusion, since the record will probably not disclose an error in complying with the requirements of offers of proof.
- By amendment on December 1, 2000, the final sentence in (a) was added. The Advisory Committee recognized that courts are in dispute over whether one must renew an objection or offer of proof at trial, if the trial court made an advanced ruling. Some courts hold that the objection or offer must be renewed to preserve a claim for appeal, and some hold that it does not. This amendment resolves the conflict and makes it clear that if the ruling is "definitive," renewal is not required.

## Rule 104. Preliminary Questions

(a) **Questions of admissibility generally.**
　　1. <u>Answering preliminary questions</u>:
　　　　a. The following preliminary questions are determined by the <u>judge</u>:
　　　　　　i.　The qualification of a person to be a witness.
　　　　　　ii.　The existence of a privilege.
　　　　　　iii.　The admissibility of evidence.
　　　　b. This is subject to subdivision (b).
　　2. <u>Applicability of the FRE</u>:
　　　　a. The judge is not bound by the rules of evidence in answering these questions.
　　　　b. <u>Exception:</u> Questions regarding **privilege**.

(b) **Relevancy conditioned on fact.**
　　If *evidence is relevant only if some factual condition is fulfilled*, the judge will admit such evidence upon/subject to the introduction of supporting evidence that the condition was fulfilled.

(c) **Hearing of jury.**
　　1. <u>Hearings on the admissibility of confessions</u> are always done without the jury present.
　　2. <u>Hearings on other preliminary matters</u> are done when:
　　　　a. The interests of justice require.
　　or　b. The accused is a witness <u>and</u> so requests.

(d) **Testimony by accused.**
　　An accused <u>cannot</u> be cross-examined on other issues of a case when testifying on a preliminary matter.

(e) **Weight and credibility.**
　　This rule does not limit the right of a party to introduce to the jury evidence relevant to <u>*weight*</u> or <u>*credibility*</u>.

---

**Summary of Advisory Committee's Notes on Rule 104**
- It is the judge's responsibility to determine whether a condition, upon which the applicability of a particular rule of evidence depends, exists.
- The judge will make the decision, whether these are factual inquiries or based on a legally set standard.
- If it is a factual inquiry, the evidence that the judge receives (pro and con on the issue) is not subject to the rules in general.
- Unlike this rule, questions of "*conditional relevancy*," or whether a preliminary fact that would determine the relevancy of evidence exists, are left for the jury (e.g., A statement spoken to provide notice to X is without probative value unless X heard it).
- The judge will make the preliminary ruling on foundation, and the evidence is admitted for the jury to evaluate. This is to be distinguished from problems of logical relevancy, which are dealt with in Rule 401.

- Subdivision (c) makes clear that preliminary hearings on the admissibility of confessions must be conducted outside the hearing of the jury. The judge, however, may use his discretion, as there are things that may be heard in front of a jury with no adverse effect.
- Subdivision (d) limits cross-examination and is designed to encourage participation by the accused in the determination of preliminary matters. The accused may testify about them without being exposed to cross-examination, which is otherwise broad (see Rule 611(b)).

## Rule 105. Limited Admissibility

a. This rule applies to evidence that is admissible:
    1. As to one party but not another party.
  or 2. For one purpose but not for another purpose.

b. When this evidence is admitted, the court shall, <u>upon request</u>:
    1. Restrict the evidence to the party or purpose (for which it was admitted).
  and 2. Instruct the jury accordingly.

**Summary of Advisory Committee's Notes on Rule 105**
This rule is similar to Rule 403, as both limit the admissibility of evidence when there is substantial risk of prejudice. Note that limiting instructions are not effective in all situations.

## Rule 106. Remainder of or Related Writings or Recorded Statements

a. <u>This rule applies to</u>:
    1. Writings.
  and 2. Recordings.
  and 3. Parts of writings/recordings.

b. When such evidence is introduced, an adverse party can require that the rest of the writing or recording (or any other writing or recording that should fairly be considered together with it) be introduced.

**Summary of Advisory Committee's Notes on Rule 106**

This rule is based on two considerations:
(1) The first is the misleading impression created by taking matters out of context.
(2) The second is the inadequacy of repair work when delayed to a point later in the trial.

Note that the adversary retains the right to examine the matter further on cross-examination or as part of her own case.

# ARTICLE II
# JUDICIAL NOTICE

## Rule 201. Judicial Notice of Adjudicative Facts

(a) **Scope of rule.**

"This rule governs only <u>judicial notice</u> of <u>adjudicative facts</u>."

(b) **Kinds of facts.**

A "judicially noticed fact" must be *a fact not subject to reasonable dispute* because:

  (1) It is generally known within the jurisdiction of the trial court.

or (2) It can be readily and accurately determined by reliable sources.

(c) **When discretionary.**

The judge has discretion to take judicial notice (regardless of whether or not a party requests it).

(d) **When mandatory.**

The judge <u>must</u> take judicial notice when:

  1. A party requests it.

and 2. The necessary information is supplied.

(e) **Opportunity to be heard.**

  1. A party is entitled to an opportunity to be heard as to:

     a. The appropriateness of taking judicial notice.

   or b. The substance of the matter noted.

  2. <u>Requirements</u>:

     a. A <u>timely request</u> must be made.

   or b. If there was no prior notification, a request must be made after judicial notice has been taken.

(f) **Time of taking notice.**

"Judicial notice may be taken *at any stage* of the proceeding."

(g) **Instructing jury.**

The court shall give the following instructions to the jury:

  1. In a **civil action or proceeding**: To accept any fact "judicially noticed" as <u>CONCLUSIVE</u>.

  2. In a **criminal case**: That it may (but is not required to) accept any fact "judicially noticed" as <u>TRUE</u>.

---

**Summary of Advisory Committee's Notes on Rule 201**

• This is the only rule that deals with judicial notice. The rule specifies *"adjudicative" facts* as opposed to *"legislative" facts*. Judicial notice of "legislative" facts is not dealt with in the rules. **Adjudicative facts** are simply the facts of the particular case. **Legislative facts** are those that have relevance to legal reasoning and the lawmaking process (whether by a court or legislative body).

- Subdivision (b) shows the caution of the rules in requiring that the matter be beyond reasonable controversy.
- It must be noted that the entire trial-type procedure is based on the taking of evidence and subjecting that evidence to rebuttal and cross-examination. This is why for judicial notice of a fact, the rules require that the fact be "so universally known that it is not subject to dispute."
- Under subdivision (c) the judge has a discretionary authority to take judicial notice, regardless of whether she is so requested by a party.
- The taking of judicial notice is <u>mandatory</u>, (under subdivision (d)), only when a party requests it and the necessary information is supplied.
- Subdivision (e) reflects that it is only fair to have an opportunity to be heard on the <u>propriety of taking judicial notice</u> and the <u>substance of the matter noticed</u>. That opportunity is granted upon request. There is, however, no formal procedure for giving an adversary advance notice that a request has been made to take judicial notice.
- According to subdivision (f), judicial notice may be taken at any time (whether in trial or on appeal).
- Finally, subdivision (g) seems to disallow evidence in disproof of facts (of which judicial notice is taken).
  - This would undermine the purposes of judicial notice. Ample opportunity to be heard is provided by subdivision (e).
  - <u>Criminal cases</u> are treated differently. This is in keeping with the general rule that a verdict cannot be directed against the accused in a criminal case (see cases for explanation).
- Note finally that the Advisory Committee chose not to treat judicial notice of law in the rules and has left the topic for treatment to the Rules of Civil and Criminal Procedure.

# ARTICLE III
# PRESUMPTIONS IN CIVIL ACTIONS AND PROCEEDINGS

## Rule 301. Presumptions in General in Civil Actions and Proceedings

a. <u>Scope of this rule</u>: All civil actions and proceedings that are not otherwise provided for by act of Congress or by the FRE.

b. **Opposing party's burden:**
    1. The opposing party has the <u>*burden of going forward*</u> with evidence that *either:*
        a. Rebuts the presumption directed to it.
    or  b. Meets the presumption directed to it.
    2. The opposing party <u>does not</u> have the <u>*burden of persuasion*</u> (which remains on the party who has the burden in the first place).

> **Summary of Advisory Committee's Notes on Rule 301**
> The presumptions governed by Rule 301 place the burden of establishing the <u>non-existence</u> of a presumed fact on the opposing party only once the party invoking the presumption establishes the basic facts giving rise to it.

## Rule 302. Applicability of State Law in Civil Actions and Proceedings

a. If a fact is an element of a state law claim or defense, state law determines the effect of the presumption.

b. This rule applies to civil actions and proceedings.

> **Summary of Advisory Committee's Notes on Rule 302**
> - Not all presumptions in diversity cases are governed by state law. This is the case only when the burden of proof has to do with a "substantive element of the claim or defense."
> - The rule does not apply state law when the presumption operates upon a lesser aspect of the case (i.e., "tactical" presumptions). Note that reference to "diversity" is not completely accurate. According to the rule, the claim or issue must have its <u>source</u> in state law. The rule would not therefore apply to <u>a federal claim or issue</u>, even though jurisdiction is based on diversity.

# ARTICLE IV
# RELEVANCY AND ITS LIMITS

## Rule 401. Definition of "Relevant Evidence"

**"Relevant evidence"** is evidence that makes a key fact either more or less likely to be true than it would have been without the evidence.

**Summary of Advisory Committee's Notes on Rule 401**

- To determine relevancy, we ask whether an item of evidence has <u>sufficient probative value</u> to justify receiving it in evidence.
- The variety of relevancy problems is proportionate to the ingenuity of counsel in using circumstantial evidence as a means of proof.
- An enormous number of cases fall in no set pattern, and this rule is designed as a guide for handling them. On the other hand, some situations are frequent and create patterns and demand treatment by specific rules, specifically Rule 404 and those following it.
- There is another concept that is worth defining here, and that is "**<u>conditional relevance</u>**." In this situation, probative value depends not only upon satisfying the basic requirement of relevancy but also upon the existence of some matter of fact (e.g., if evidence of a spoken statement is relied upon to prove notice, there is no probative value unless the person sought to be charged heard the statement).
- The problem is one of fact, and the only rules needed are for the purpose of determining the respective functions of judge and jury. See Rules 104(b) and 901.
- In determining relevancy, we ask, "Does the item of evidence tend to prove the matter sought to be proved?"
- The answer to this depends on principles evolved by experience or science, applied logically to the situation at hand (see James, Relevancy, Probability and the Law, 29 Cal. L. Rev. 689, 696, n.15 (1941), in Selected Writings on Evidence and Trial 610, 615, n.15 (Fryer ed. 1957)).
- The standard of probability under the rule is "more * * * probable than it would be without the evidence." Any more stringent requirement is unrealistic.
- Dealing with probability in the language of the rule avoids confusion between questions of admissibility and questions of the sufficiency of the evidence.
- The rule uses the phrase "fact that is of consequence to the determination of the action" to describe the kind of fact to which proof may properly be directed. The fact to be proved may be <u>ultimate</u>, <u>intermediate</u>, or <u>evidentiary</u>; it does not matter, as long as it helps in the determination of the action.
- The fact to which the evidence is directed need not be in dispute. Evidence that is essentially background in nature (e.g. charts, photographs, views of real estate, murder weapons, and others) rarely involves disputed matter, yet it is always offered and admitted to aid understanding.
- A rule limiting admissibility to evidence directed to a controversial point would risk the exclusion of this helpful evidence, or at least the raising of endless questions over its admission.

## Rule 402. Relevant Evidence Generally Admissible; Irrelevant Evidence Inadmissible

a. All **relevant evidence** is <u>admissible,</u> *unless* otherwise provided by:
   1. The U.S. Constitution.
   or 2. An act of Congress.
   or 3. The FRE.
   or 4. Other rules prescribed by the U.S. Supreme Court pursuant to statutory authority.

b. Evidence that is **not relevant** is <u>inadmissible</u>.

---

**Summary of Advisory Committee's Notes on Rule 402**

- The provisions that state that <u>all relevant evidence is admissible (with certain exceptions)</u>, and that <u>evidence that is not relevant is not admissible</u> "*constitute the foundation upon which the structure of admission and exclusion rests.*"
- Not all relevant evidence, however, is admissible.
- The exclusion of relevant evidence occurs in a variety of situations (which are called for by these rules, the Rules of Civil and Criminal Procedure, Bankruptcy Rules, by act of Congress, or by constitutional considerations).
- The following rules in Article 4, in response to the demands of particular policies, require the exclusion of evidence despite its relevancy.
- In addition, Article 5 recognizes a number of privileges.
- Article 6 imposes limitations upon witnesses and the manner of dealing with them.
- Article 7 specifies requirements with respect to opinions and expert testimony.
- Article 8 excludes hearsay not falling within an exception.
- Article 9 spells out the handling of authentication and identification.
- Article 10 restricts the manner of proving the contents of writings and recordings.
  - **Examples of exclusion of relevant evidence in the Rules of Civil and Criminal Procedure:**
    (a) Rules 30(b) and 32(a)(3) of the Rules of Civil Procedure, by imposing requirements of notice and unavailability of the deponent, place limits on the use of relevant depositions.
    (b) Rule 15 of the Rules of Criminal Procedure restricts the use of depositions in criminal cases, even though relevant.
    (c) Rule 5(a) of the Rules of Criminal Procedure, where an arrested person must be taken without unnecessary delay before a commissioner (or other similar officer) is held to require the exclusion of statements elicited during detention in violation of the rule (citation omitted). Evidence excluded by congressional act consists mostly of legislation that provides for the formulation of a privilege or of a prohibition against disclosure.
- Two examples of constitutional considerations that impose basic limitations upon the admissibility of relevant evidence are evidence obtained by unlawful search and seizure and incriminating statements elicited from an accused in violation of the right to counsel.

# Rule 403. Exclusion of Relevant Evidence on Grounds of Prejudice, Confusion, or Waste of Time

Relevant evidence may be excluded if its value is substantially outweighed by *either*:

   1. <u>The danger of</u>:
-      a. Unfair prejudice.
- or  b. Confusion of the issues.
- or  c. Misleading the jury.

or  2. <u>Considerations of</u>:
-      a. Undue delay.
- or  b. Waste of time.
- or  c. Needless presentation of cumulative evidence.

---

**Summary of Advisory Committee's Notes on Rule 403**

- The case law recognizes that in certain circumstances the exclusion of evidence that is of unquestioned relevance is called for (e.g., the risks in admitting the evidence range from inducing decision on a purely emotional basis to merely wasting time, at the other extreme). Situations like this call for balancing the probative value of the evidence against the harm likely to result from its admission.
- The following rules in Article 4 are concrete applications for particular situations. However, they are based on the policies underlying the present rule, which is designed as a guide for handling situations that have no specific rule.
- ***"Unfair prejudice"*** within its context means an <u>undue tendency to suggest decision</u> on an improper basis (usually an emotional one).
- The rule does not list "surprise" as a ground for exclusion. There are three likely reasons for this rule:
  - (1) It is usually "coupled with the danger of prejudice and confusion of issues" (citation omitted).
  - (2) The impact of a rule excluding evidence on the ground of surprise would be difficult to estimate.
  - (3) The granting of a continuance is a better procedural tool than exclusion.
- In reaching a decision whether or not to exclude evidence on grounds of <u>unfair prejudice</u>, consideration should be given to the *probable effectiveness* or *lack of effectiveness* of a <u>limiting instruction</u>. (See Rule 105).
- The availability of other means of proof may also be an appropriate factor.

---

# Rule 404. Character Evidence Not Admissible to Prove Conduct; Exceptions; Other Crimes

(a) **Character evidence generally.**
   1. "Character evidence" is evidence of a person's character or character trait.
   2. <u>Admissibility</u>:
-      a. Character evidence is <u>not admissible</u> to prove that a person acted in keeping with that character.

b. **Exceptions** (The following character evidence may be admitted):

(1) <u>**Character of accused (in a criminal case)**</u> if:

    a. The evidence is <u>offered by the accused</u> and is pertinent.

or  b. The evidence is <u>offered by the prosecution to rebut</u> character evidence offered by the accused.

or  c. The evidence is offered by the prosecution to show the character trait of the accused, <u>where the accused offers the character trait of the alleged victim</u> (under Rule 404(a)(2)), and the evidence is admitted.

(2) <u>**Character of the alleged victim (in a criminal case and subject to Rule 412 (sex offense cases)**</u>*), if:

    a. The evidence is <u>offered by the accused</u> and is pertinent.

or  b. The evidence is <u>offered by the prosecution to rebut</u> character evidence offered by the accused.

or  c. The evidence is offered in a <u>homicide case and is:</u>

      i. Offered by the prosecution.

and  ii. Offered to show the peacefulness of the alleged victim of the homicide.

and  iii. Used to rebut evidence that the alleged victim was the aggressor.

(3) Character of the witness. (See Rules 607, 608 and 609).

(b) **Admissibility of evidence of other crimes, wrongs, or acts.**

1. Evidence of a person's other crimes, wrongs, or acts is <u>not</u> admissible to prove that the person acted *in keeping with that character.*

2. <u>Exceptions:</u>

    a. Such evidence may be admissible for other purposes, such as proof of:

      1. Motive.

      2. Opportunity.

      3. Intent.

      4. Preparation.

      5. Plan.

      6. Knowledge.

      7. Identity.

      8. Absence of mistake or accident.

    b. <u>Requirement</u> (in a criminal case): Upon request of the accused, the prosecution must provide *reasonable notice* of the general nature of the evidence, *either:*

      i. <u>Before</u> trial.

or  ii. <u>During</u> trial, if the court excuses pretrial notice on good cause shown.

---

*In a criminal case involving sexual misconduct, the admissibility of evidence of the victim's sexual behavior/predisposition is governed by Rule 412, which is more stringent.

**Summary of Advisory Committee's Notes on Rule 404**

- Subdivision (a) deals with the basic question whether **character evidence** should be admitted.
  - Once the admissibility of character evidence is established under this rule one must refer to Rule 405 to determine the <u>appropriate method of proof</u>.
  - If the character is that of a witness, see Rules 608 and 610 for methods of proof.
- Character questions arise in two fundamentally different ways:
  (1) Character may itself be an element of a <u>crime</u>, <u>claim</u>, or <u>defense</u> (this situation is commonly referred to as "character in issue").
     <u>Examples are</u>:
     - The chastity of the victim under a statute specifying her chastity as an element of the crime of seduction.
     - The competency of the driver in an action for negligently entrusting a motor vehicle to an incompetent driver.
     - The present rule has no provision on the subject of general relevancy, as there is no problem in that regard. The only question relates to <u>allowable methods of proof</u>, which is dealt with in Rule 405.
  (2) Character evidence is susceptible of being used to suggest that the person acted on the occasion in question consistently with his character (often described as "circumstantial").
     <u>Examples are</u>:
     (a)  evidence of a violent disposition to prove that the person was the aggressor in an affray.
     (b)  evidence of honesty in disproof of a charge of theft.
- This circumstantial use of character evidence raises questions of relevancy as well as questions of allowable methods of proof.
- In most jurisdictions today, the circumstantial use of character is rejected but with three important exceptions incorporated in the rule.
- A provision similar to the limitation to pertinent traits of character in paragraphs (1) and (2) (rather than character generally) exists in Rule 608 (referred to in paragraph (3)), which limits character evidence respecting witnesses to the trait of truthfulness or untruthfulness.
- The argument is made that circumstantial use of character ought to be allowed in civil cases to the same extent as in criminal cases (i.e., evidence of good (non-prejudicial) character would be admissible in the first instance, subject to rebuttal by evidence of bad character).
- The difficulty with expanding the use of character evidence in civil cases is that "character evidence is of slight probative value and may be very prejudicial. It tends to distract the trier of fact from the main question of what actually happened on the particular occasion. It subtly permits the trier of fact to reward the good man and punish the bad man because of their respective characters despite what the evidence in the case shows actually happened" (see California Law Revision Commission).
- Subdivision (b) deals with an application of the general rule excluding <u>circumstantial use of character evidence</u>.

- Evidence of other crimes, wrongs, or acts is not admissible to prove character as a basis for suggesting that conduct on a particular occasion was in conformity with it. This is consistent with the general rule.
- However, this type of evidence may be offered for another purpose that does not fall within the prohibition (e.g., proof of motive, opportunity). The determination must be made whether *the danger of undue prejudice outweighs the probative value of the evidence* in view of the availability of other means of proof and other factors appropriate for making decisions of this kind under Rule 403.
- The major change made by a December 1, 2000, amendment was that an accused cannot attack the alleged victim's character and yet remain shielded from the same evidence concerning himself. Originally, an accused could offer proof of self-defense by offering proof of the alleged victim's violent character. The alleged victim could only then show his character for peacefulness, and could not show the accused's character for violence. Also, the word "alleged" was added to the term "victim" in Rule 404(a)(2) (this is to be consistent with Rule 412).
- In 2006 the rule was amended to clarify that in a <u>civil case</u>, evidence of a person's character is <u>never</u> admissible to prove that the person acted in conformity with the character trait. (There had been an ongoing dispute in the case law as to whether the exceptions in 404 (a)(1) and (2) permit the circumstantial use of character evidence in civil cases.)

## Rule 405. Methods of Proving Character

(a) **Reputation or opinion.**
> 1. In cases where character evidence is <u>admissible</u>, proof may be made by:
> > a. Testimony as to reputation.
> > or   b. Testimony in the form of an opinion.
> 2. *Specific instances of conduct* may be explored as proof on cross-examination.

(b) **Specific instances of conduct.**
> 1. *Specific instances of conduct* may also be used as proof where a person's character/character trait is an <u>essential element</u> of a charge, claim, or defense.

**Summary of Advisory Committee's Notes on Rule 405**
- This rule does not deal with the admissibility of character evidence (which is dealt with in Rule 404). This rule deals only with <u>allowable methods of proving character</u>.
- The most convincing of the three methods provided is <u>evidence of specific conduct</u>, which, on the other hand, can give rise to the most prejudice, confusion, surprise, and consumption of time. That is why the rule limits the use of this type of evidence in subsection (b).
- Specific instances of conduct may also be inquired about on cross-examination of a witness testifying on opinion or reputation.
  - This is meant to "shed light" on the accuracy of a witness's hearing and reporting.

- This type of testimony is not generally permissible on direct examination of an ordinary opinion witness to character.
- The rule with regard to <u>opinion evidence</u> is based on earlier practice that permitted opinion evidence and argument for evidence based on personal knowledge and belief.

## Rule 406. Habit; Routine Practice

a. <u>Evidence admissible</u>:
  1. A person's habit.
  or 2. The routine practice of an organization.

b. <u>Relevance</u>: The evidence is relevant to prove that certain conduct was in keeping with that habit or routine.

c. The evidence is admissible <u>regardless</u> of:
  1. Whether the evidence has been corroborated.
  or 2. The presence of eyewitnesses.

**Summary of Advisory Committee's Notes on Rule 406**
- The notes indicate that <u>habit</u> is different from character in that it is more specific (quoting McCormick). While character describes a tendency to do certain things, habit describes an actual regular practice.
- Habit evidence is considered highly persuasive as proof of conduct on a particular occasion. The question of how consistent and often behavior must take place to constitute a habit has given rise to differences of opinion. Specific standards cannot be formulated.
- Religious habits have generally been held to be inadmissible as evidence given the "volitional basis" of religious activity. There is a trend towards admitting evidence of a routine of business dealings to prove the same deal or bargain had occurred.

## Rule 407. Subsequent Remedial Measures
(Effective December 1, 1997)

*This rule was amended to include product liability actions in the exclusionary principle. It was also amended to clarify that the rule applies only to remedial measures made <u>after</u> the occurrence that caused the damages.*

a. A **"subsequent remedial measure"** is:
  1. A measure that is taken after injury or harm caused by an event.
  and 2. A measure that would have made the injury or harm less likely to occur had it been taken earlier.

b. Evidence of **subsequent remedial measures** taken is:
  1. <u>Inadmissible</u> to prove:
      a. Negligence.
      or b. Culpable conduct.
      or c. A defect in a product.

or   d. A defect in a product's design.

or   e. A need for a warning or instruction.

but 2. **Admissible** for other purposes, like proving:

     a. Ownership.

or   b. Control.

or   c. Feasibility of precautionary measures (if disputed).

or   d. Impeachment.

---

**Summary of Advisory Committee's Notes on Rule 407**

- This rule not allowing evidence of subsequent remedial measures as an admission of fault is based on two things:
  - (1) The conduct is really not a good indicator of fault since it may be in response to a mere accident or contributory negligence.
  - (2) There is a social policy of encouraging people to take steps in furtherance of added safety.
- Some examples of <u>subsequent conduct</u> are repairs, installation of safety devices, changes in company rules, and discharge of employees.
- The second sentence of the rule addresses the limitation and allows the evidence to be admitted for other purposes.

---

# Rule 408. Compromise and Offers to Compromise

1. This rule applies to evidence of:

    (a)(1) Giving or receiving (or offering or promising to give or receive) valuable consideration in a compromise/attempt to compromise a claim.

or  (a)(2) <u>Conduct</u> at compromise negotiations (regarding the claim) or a <u>statement</u> made in compromise negotiations (regarding the claim).

*Admissible or Inadmissible?*

a. **Inadmissible**.

    1. If used to prove <u>liability</u> for or <u>invalidity</u> of a disputed claim or its amount.

or  2. If used to impeach a prior inconsistent statement (or contradiction).

b. **Admissible** for other purposes, like:

    a. Proving bias of a witness.

    b. Negating a contention of undue delay.

    c. Proving an effort to obstruct a criminal investigation or prosecution.

**Summary of Advisory Committee's Notes on Rule 408**

- Evidence of an offer to compromise a claim is not receivable in evidence as an admission of the validity or invalidity of the claim.
- As with evidence of subsequent remedial measures (Rule 407) this is based on two grounds:
  (1) The evidence is irrelevant, since the offer may be motivated by a desire for peace rather than from any concession of weakness of position.
  (2) Promotion of the public policy favoring the compromise and settlement of disputes.
- The same policy underlies Rule 68 of the Federal Rules of Civil Procedure, where evidence of an unaccepted offer of judgment is not admissible except in a proceeding to determine costs.
- Under present law, however, in most jurisdictions statements of fact made during settlement negotiations are excepted from this ban and are admissible. This inhibits freedom of communication with respect to compromise, even among lawyers.
- The only escape from admissibility of statements of fact made in a settlement negotiation is if:
  (1) The declarant or her representative expressly states that the statement is hypothetical, stated to be "without prejudice."
  (2) The statement is so connected with the offer as to be inseparable from it.
- Another effect is the controversy over whether a given statement falls within or without the protected area. These considerations account for the expansion of the rule to include evidence of conduct or statements made in compromise negotiations, as well as the offer or completed compromise itself.
- Finally, since the rule excludes only when the purpose is proving the validity or invalidity of the claim or its amount, an offer for another purpose is not within the rule.
- Under existing federal law evidence of conduct and statements made in compromise negotiations is admissible in subsequent litigation between the parties. Admissions of liability or opinions given during compromise negotiations are inadmissible, but evidence of unqualified factual assertions is admissible.

## Rule 409. Payment of Medical and Similar Expenses

Evidence of an offer or promise to pay medical, hospital, or other expenses, or actually paying such expenses, that arose as a result of an injury is inadmissible to prove liability for the injury.

**Summary of Advisory Committee's Notes on Rule 409**

- The considerations underlying this rule parallel those underlying Rules 407 (subsequent remedial measures) and Rule 408 (offers of compromise).
- "[G]enerally, evidence of payment of medical, hospital, or similar expenses of an injured party by the opposing party, is not admissible, the reason often given being that such payment or offer is usually made from humane impulses and not from an admission of liability, and that to hold otherwise would tend to discourage assistance to the injured person."

- Unlike Rule 408 (offers of compromise), this rule does not extend to conduct or statements not a part of the act of furnishing or offering or promising to pay. This difference arises from fundamental differences in nature. Communication is necessary if compromises are to take place, and consequently broad protection of statements is needed. This is not so in cases of payments or offers or promises to pay medical expenses, where factual statements may be expected to be incidental in nature.

## Rule 410. Inadmissibility of Pleas, Plea Discussions, and Related Statements

a. <u>Scope</u>: This rule applies to both civil and criminal proceedings.

b. Except as otherwise provided, the following is <u>inadmissible</u> against a defendant who either made a plea or participated in plea discussions:

    (1) Evidence that a guilty plea was later withdrawn.

    (2) Evidence of a *nolo contendere* plea.

    (3) Any statement made in the course of the proceeding under (Federal Rule of Criminal Procedure 11 or comparable state rule) regarding (1) or (2).

    (4) Evidence of <u>plea statements</u>:

        a. Any statement made in the course of plea discussions with a prosecutor that either:

            i. Did not result in a guilty plea.

        or  ii. Resulted in a guilty plea that was later withdrawn.

        b. <u>Exceptions</u>: Plea statements are <u>admissible</u> if either:

            i. Another statement made in the plea discussions has been introduced (and it is only fair if this statement is considered together with it).

        or  ii. In a <u>criminal proceeding for perjury or false statement</u>, where:

                1. The defendant was under oath.

            and 2. The statement was on the record.

            and 3. The statement was made in front of counsel.

**Summary of Advisory Committee's Notes on Rule 410**

- *History*: Withdrawn pleas of guilty were held inadmissible in federal prosecutions in <u>Kercheval v. United States</u>, 274 U.S. 220 (1927). The Court stated that to admit the withdrawn plea would effectively negate the allowance of withdrawal and place the accused in a dilemma inconsistent with the decision to award him a trial. The New York Court of Appeals, in <u>People v. Spitaleri</u>, 212 N.Y.S.2d 53 (1961), reexamined and overturned its earlier decisions that had allowed admission. In addition to the reasons set forth in <u>Kercheval</u>, which was quoted at length, the court pointed out that admitting the plea would force the defendant to take the stand (by explaining) and allow the way for the prosecution to call the lawyer who had represented him at the time of entering the plea.

- The present rule seeks to avoid the admission of guilt that is inherent in pleas of guilty (See Rule 11 of the Rules of Criminal Procedure, which recognizes *nolo contendere* pleas). The purpose of excluding offers to plead guilty or *nolo contendere* is the promotion of disposition of criminal cases by compromise.
- The exclusionary rule is limited to <u>use against the accused</u>. This is consistent with the purpose of the rule, since the possibility of use for or against other persons will not impair the effectiveness of withdrawing pleas or the freedom of discussion that the rule promotes.

## Rule 411. Liability Insurance

Evidence concerning whether or not someone is insured for liability is:

  a. **Inadmissible** to prove negligence or another wrongful act.
  b. **Admissible** for other purposes, like:
    i. Proof of agency, ownership, or control.
    ii. Proof of bias or prejudice of a witness.

**Summary of Advisory Committee's Notes on Rule 411**

- The courts have rejected evidence of liability insurance for the purpose of proving fault, and absence of liability insurance as proof of lack of fault. This takes into account the feeling that knowledge of the presence or absence of liability insurance would induce juries to decide cases on improper grounds.
- The rule is drafted in broad terms so as to include contributory negligence or other fault of a plaintiff as well as fault of a defendant.
- The second sentence points out the limits of the rule, using well-established illustrations.

## Rule 412. Sex Offense Cases; Relevance of Victim's Past Behavior

(a) **Reputation** or **opinion evidence** of the alleged victim's (of an 18 U.S.C. Chapter 109A offense) past sexual behavior is <u>inadmissible</u>.

(b) Evidence about the alleged victim's past sexual behavior (other than reputation or opinion evidence) is also <u>inadmissible</u> *unless:*
    (1) It is admitted in accordance with 412(c)(1) <u>and</u> 412(c)(2) <u>and</u> is constitutionally required to be admitted.
  or (2) It is admitted in accordance with 412(c) <u>and</u> is evidence of *either:*
    (A) Past sexual behavior with someone other than the accused, <u>and</u> is offered by the accused to show that he was not the source of semen or of the victim's injury.
    or (B) Past sexual behavior with the accused, <u>and</u> is offered by the accused to show that the victim consented to the sexual behavior at issue.

(c) **Motion and hearing.**
   (1) <u>Motion</u>: In order to offer evidence under 412(b) (regarding the victim's past sexual behavior), an accused must make a motion:
       a. <u>In writing.</u>
       and b. <u>In a timely manner</u>.
           1. Not later than <u>15 days</u> before the date the trial is scheduled to begin.
           or 2. The court may allow the motion to be made at a later date (including during trial) if:
               i. The evidence is newly discovered <u>and</u> could not have been obtained earlier with *due diligence*.
               or ii. The evidence relates to an issue that recently arose.
       and c. Serve the motion on the alleged victim and on all other parties.
   (2) <u>Hearing</u>:
       a. The (c)(1) motion must be accompanied by a <u>written offer of proof</u>.
       b. If the court determines that it satisfies (b), the court shall order a hearing to decide the admissibility of the evidence.
       c. Witnesses (including the alleged victim) and relevant evidence may be introduced at the hearing.
       d. If the relevancy of the evidence depends on the fulfillment of a condition, the court may hear evidence on whether that condition has been fulfilled.
   (3) The evidence is <u>admissible</u> at trial if:
       a. <u>The court</u> (at the hearing) <u>determines that</u>:
           i. The evidence is relevant.
           and ii. Its value outweighs the danger of unfair prejudice.
       and b. <u>A court order is made, specifying</u>:
           i. What evidence may be offered.
           and ii. In what areas the victim may be examined and cross-examined.

(d) **"Past sexual behavior"** is sexual behavior other than the sexual behavior involved in the allegation.

---

**Summary of Advisory Committee's Notes on Rule 412**
- The purpose of Rule 412 is to protect the alleged victim against the <u>invasion of privacy</u>, <u>potential embarrassment,</u> and <u>sexual stereotyping</u> that is associated with public disclosure of intimate sexual details in the factfinding process.
- The rule also encourages victims of sexual misconduct to institute and to participate in legal proceedings against alleged offenders. Rule 412 seeks to do this by not allowing evidence relating to the alleged victim's sexual behavior or alleged sexual predisposition (whether offered as substantive evidence or for

impeachment) except in designated cases in which the *probative value of the evidence significantly outweighs possible harm to the victim.*

- The rule applies in all cases involving sexual misconduct regardless of whether the *alleged victim* or person accused is a party to the litigation. The term "*alleged victim*" is used because there will frequently be a factual dispute as to whether sexual misconduct occurred. It does not mean that the misconduct had to be alleged in the pleadings.

- The person against whom the evidence is offered, however, must reasonably be characterized as a "*victim of alleged sexual misconduct.*" When this is not the case (e.g., a defamation action involving statements concerning sexual misconduct in which the evidence is offered to show that the alleged defamatory statements were true or did not damage the plaintiff's reputation) neither Rule 404 nor this rule will operate to bar the evidence; Rule 401 and 403 will continue to control.

- The reference to a person "accused" is also nontechnical. There is no requirement that there be a criminal charge pending against the person or even that the misconduct would constitute a criminal offense. Evidence offered to prove allegedly false prior claims by the victim is not barred by Rule 412. However, this evidence is subject to the requirements of Rule 404.

- In subdivision (a), "*past sexual behavior*" refers to all activities that involve actual physical conduct (i.e., sexual intercourse and sexual contact), or that imply sexual intercourse or sexual contact (e.g., use of contraceptives, birth of an illegitimate child, evidence of venereal disease inadmissible).

- Evidence relating to the alleged victim's mode of dress, speech, or lifestyle will not be admissible, unless the exception in (b)(2) is satisfied, since admission of that evidence would go against Rule 412's objectives.

- Rule 412 applies to both civil and criminal proceedings.

- The reason for extending the rule to all criminal cases is the strong social policy of protecting a victim's privacy and encouraging victims to come forward to report criminal acts.

- The reason for extending Rule 412 to civil cases is the need to protect alleged victims against invasions of privacy, potential embarrassment, and unwarranted sexual stereotyping. The wish to encourage victims to come forward when they have been sexually molested does not disappear because the claim has shifted from a criminal prosecution to a claim for damages or injunctive relief. There is a strong social policy in not only punishing those who engage in sexual misconduct, but in also providing relief to the victim. Thus, Rule 412 applies in any civil case in which a person claims to be the victim of sexual misconduct (e.g., sexual battery, sexual harassment).

- Subdivision (b) spells out the specific circumstances in which some evidence that would otherwise be barred by the general rule may be admissible. In a criminal case, evidence may be admitted under subdivision (b)(1) pursuant to three possible exceptions, if the evidence also satisfies other requirements for admissibility specified in the Federal Rules of Evidence, including Rule 403.

  - Subdivisions (b)(1)(A) and (b)(1)(B) require proof in the form of specific instances of sexual behavior. This is because evidence of reputation or evidence in the form of an opinion has limited probative value and reliability.

  - Under subdivision (b)(1)(A), evidence of specific instances of sexual behavior (with persons other than the person whose sexual misconduct is alleged) may be admissible if it is offered to prove that another person was the <u>source of semen</u>, <u>injury,</u> or <u>other physical evidence</u>.

- Where the prosecution has directly or indirectly asserted that the physical evidence originated with the accused, the defendant must have an opportunity to prove that another person was responsible.

- Under the exception in subdivision (b)(1)(B), evidence of specific instances of sexual behavior with respect to the person whose sexual misconduct is alleged is admissible if offered to prove <u>consent</u>, or offered by the prosecution. This might include evidence of prior instances of sexual activities between the alleged victim and the accused, as well as statements in which the alleged victim expressed an intent to engage in sexual intercourse with the accused or voiced sexual fantasies involving the specific accused.

- In a prosecution for child sexual abuse, for example, evidence of uncharged sexual activity between the accused and the alleged victim offered by the prosecution may be admissible pursuant to Rule 404(b) to show a pattern of behavior. Evidence relating to the victim's alleged sexual predisposition is not admissible pursuant to this exception.

- Under subdivision (b)(1)(C), evidence of specific instances of conduct may not be excluded if it would deny a criminal defendant constitutional protections. For example, statements in which the victim has expressed an intent to have sex with the first person encountered on a particular occasion might not be excluded without violating the due process right of a rape defendant seeking to prove consent.

- Subdivision (b)(2) uses a <u>balancing test</u> rather than the specific exceptions stated in subdivision (b)(1) because of the difficulty of foreseeing future developments in the law. The balancing test requires the proponent of the evidence, whether plaintiff or defendant, to convince the court that the probative value of the proffered evidence *"substantially outweighs the danger of harm to any victim and of unfair prejudice of any party."* This test differs in three ways from the general rule governing admissibility (Rule 403):

   (1) It shifts the burden to the proponent to show admissibility rather than making the opponent justify exclusion of the evidence.

   (2) The standard in subdivision (b)(2) is more stringent than in the original rule; it raises the threshold for admission by requiring that the probative value of the evidence substantially outweigh the specified dangers.

   (3) Rule 412's test puts *"harm to the victim"* on the scale in addition to prejudice to the parties.

# Rule 412. Sex Offense Cases; Relevance of Victim's Past Behavior or Alleged Sexual Predisposition

*Rule 412 as <u>amended</u> by the Violent Crime Control Act, 1994.*

(a) **Evidence generally inadmissible**. The following is <u>not admissible</u> in any civil or criminal proceeding involving alleged sexual misconduct (see exceptions in (b) and (c)):

   (1) Evidence offered to prove that any alleged victim engaged in *other* sexual behavior.

(2) Evidence offered to prove any alleged victim's "sexual predisposition."

(b) **Exceptions**

    (1) <u>Criminal case</u>: The following is admissible in a <u>criminal case</u> (if otherwise admissible):

        (A) Evidence of specific instances of sexual behavior by the alleged victim that is offered to prove that someone other than the accused was the source of semen, injury, or other physical evidence.

        (B) Evidence of specific instances of sexual behavior by the alleged victim (with respect to the person accused) that is offered by:

            1. The accused to prove consent.

          or 2. The prosecution.

        (C) Evidence that if excluded would violate the defendant's constitutional rights.

    (2) <u>Civil case</u>: The following is admissible in a <u>civil case</u>:

        a. Evidence offered to prove **sexual behavior/predisposition** of any alleged victim is admissible if:

            1. Otherwise admissible under the FRE.

         and 2. Its probative value *substantially outweighs* the danger of harm to any victim and of unfair prejudice to any party.

        b. Evidence of an alleged victim's **reputation** *only if* it has been placed in controversy by the alleged victim.

(c) **Procedure to determine admissibility.**

    (1) <u>Requirements of the proponent</u>: Someone who wishes to offer evidence under one of the 412(b) exceptions must:

        (A) **File a motion:**

            1. In writing.

         and 2. At least <u>14 days</u> before trial (unless the court, for good cause, requires a different time or allows during trial).

         and 3. Specifically describing the evidence.

         and 4. Stating the purpose for which it is offered.

    and (B) **Serve the motion** on all parties and notify the alleged victim (or the alleged victim's representative or guardian when appropriate).

    (2) <u>Requirements of the court</u>:

        a. The court must conduct a hearing in camera and give the alleged victim and parties a right to be heard <u>before trial</u>.

        b. The court must seal the motion, related papers, and the record of the hearing (it may order otherwise).

### Summary of Advisory Committee's Notes on Rule 412

- Rule 412 has been revised to reduce some of the confusion of the original rule and to expand the protection of alleged victims of sexual misconduct. Rule 412 applies to both civil and criminal proceedings. The goal of the rule is to protect the alleged victim against the invasion of privacy, potential embarrassment, and sexual stereotyping that usually comes with public disclosure of sexual details. By protecting victims in most instances, the rule also encourages victims of sexual misconduct to participate in legal proceedings against alleged offenders.

- The rule has been amended to also exclude all other evidence relating to an alleged victim of sexual misconduct that is offered to prove a sexual predisposition. This amendment is designed to exclude evidence that does not directly refer to sexual activities or thoughts but that the proponent believes may have a sexual connotation for the factfinder. Admission of this evidence would go against the rule's objectives of protecting the alleged victim from potential embarrassment and against stereotypical thinking. Consequently, unless the (b)(2) exception is satisfied, evidence such as that relating to the alleged victim's mode of dress, speech, or lifestyle will not be admissible.

- Amended subdivision (c) is more concise and understandable than the subdivision it replaces. The requirement of a motion before trial and the provision that a late motion may be permitted for good cause shown are continued in the amended rule. In deciding whether to permit late filing, the court may take into account the conditions previously included in the rule: (1) whether the evidence is newly discovered and could not have been obtained earlier through the existence of due diligence, and (2) whether the issue to which such evidence relates has newly arisen in the case.

- The rule recognizes that in some instances the circumstances that justify an application to introduce evidence otherwise barred by Rule 412 will not become apparent until trial.

- The amended rule provides that before admitting evidence that falls within the prohibition of Rule 412(a), the court must hold a hearing in camera at which the alleged victim and any party must be afforded the right to be present and an opportunity to be heard. All papers connected with the motion and any record of a hearing on the motion must be kept and remain under seal during the course of trial and appellate proceedings unless otherwise ordered. This is to assure the privacy of the alleged victim in all cases in which the court rules that evidence is not admissible and in which the hearing refers to matters that are not received or are received in another form.

- The procedures set forth in subdivision (c) do not apply to discovery of a victim's past sexual conduct or predisposition in civil cases, which will continue to be governed by Federal Rule of Civil Procedure 26. In order not to undermine the rationale of Rule 412, however, courts should enter appropriate orders pursuant to Federal Rule of Civil Procedure 26(c) to protect the victim against unwarranted inquiries and to ensure confidentiality. Courts should presumptively issue protective orders barring discovery unless the party seeking discovery makes a showing that the evidence sought to be discovered would be relevant under the facts and theories of the particular case and cannot be obtained except through discovery.

- One substantive change made in subdivision (c) is the elimination of the following sentence: "Notwithstanding subdivision (b) of Rule 104, if the relevancy of the evidence which the accused seeks to offer in the trial depends upon the fulfillment of a condition of fact, the court, at the hearing in chambers or at a subsequent hearing in chambers scheduled for such purpose, shall accept evidence on the issue of whether such condition of fact is fulfilled and shall determine such issue." On its face, this language appears to authorize a trial judge to exclude evidence of past sexual conduct between an alleged victim and an accused or a defendant in a civil case based upon the judge's belief that such past acts did not occur. Such an authorization raises questions of invasion of the right to a jury trial under the Sixth and Seventh Amendments.

- The Advisory Committee concluded that the amended rule provided adequate protection for all persons claiming to be the victims of sexual misconduct, and that it was inadvisable to continue to include a provision in the rule that has been confusing and that raises substantial constitutional issues.

- This section, which modifies Rule 412 of the Federal Rules of Evidence as transmitted to the Congress by the U.S. Supreme Court, is enacted pursuant to the "Rules Enabling Act."

## RULE 413. Evidence of Similar Crimes in Sexual Assault Cases

*Rule 413 as <u>added</u> by the Violent Crime Control Act, 1994.*

(a) **Admissibility of evidence of similar crimes.**
    1. <u>Type of evidence admissible</u>: Evidence that the defendant committed another offense of sexual assault (the evidence is admissible, and may be considered on any relevant matter).
    2. <u>When admissible</u>: In a criminal case in which the defendant is accused of an offense of sexual assault.

(b) **Requirements for the government when it intends to offer evidence under this rule**.
    1. <u>Requirement</u>: The attorney for the government must disclose the evidence to the defendant, including statements of witnesses or a summary of any testimony that is expected to be offered.
    2. <u>Time limit</u>:
        a. At least <u>15 days</u> before the scheduled date of trial.
    or b. At such later time as the court may allow for *good cause*.

(c) This rule shall not be construed to limit the admission or consideration of evidence under any other rule.

(d) **"Offense of sexual assault."** For purposes of this rule and Rule 415, "offense of sexual assault" means a crime under federal law or the law of a state (as defined in 18 U.S.C. § 513) that involves:
    (1) Any conduct proscribed by 18 U.S.C. Chapter 109A.
    or (2) Contact, without consent, between any part of the defendant's body or an object and the genitals or anus of another person.
    or (3) Contact, without consent, between the genitals or anus of the defendant and any part of another person's body.

or  (4) Deriving sexual pleasure or gratification from the infliction of death, bodily injury, or physical pain on another person.

or  (5) An attempt or conspiracy to engage in conduct described in paragraphs (1)-(4).

## Rule 414. Evidence of Similar Crimes in Child Molestation Cases

*Rule 414 as <u>added</u> by the Violent Crime Control Act, 1994.*

(a) **Admissibility of evidence of similar crimes.**

1. <u>Type of evidence admissible</u>: Evidence that the defendant committed another offense of child molestation (the evidence is admissible, and may be considered on any relevant matter).

2. <u>When admissible</u>: In a criminal case in which the defendant is accused of an offense of child molestation.

(b) **Requirements for the government when it intends to offer evidence under this rule**.

1. <u>Requirement</u>: The attorney for the government must disclose the evidence to the defendant, including statements of witnesses or a summary of any testimony that is expected to be offered.

2. <u>Time limit</u>:

    a. At least <u>15 days</u> before the scheduled date of trial.

or  b. At such later time as the court may allow for *good cause*.

(c) This rule shall not be construed to limit the admission or consideration of evidence under any other rule.

(d) **Definitions**. For purposes of this rule and Rule 415, **"child"** means a person below the age of 14, and **"offense of child molestation"** means a crime under federal law or the law of a state (as defined in 18 U.S.C. § 513) that involves:

(1) Any conduct proscribed by 18 U.S.C. Chapter 109A that was committed in relation to a child.

or  (2) Any conduct proscribed by 18 U.S.C. Chapter 110.

or  (3) Contact between any part of the defendant's body or an object and the genitals or anus of a child.

or  (4) Contact between the genitals or anus of the defendant and any part of the body of a child.

or  (5) Deriving sexual pleasure or gratification from the infliction of death, bodily injury, or physical pain on a child.

or  (6) An attempt or conspiracy to engage in conduct described in paragraphs (1)-(5).

## Rule 415. Evidence of Similar Acts in Civil Cases Concerning Sexual Assault or Child Molestation

*Rule 415 as <u>added</u> by the Violent Crime Control Act, 1994.*

(a) **Admissibility of evidence of similar crimes in civil cases**.

    1. <u>Type of evidence admissible</u>: Evidence of a party's commission of another offense of sexual assault or child molestation (the evidence is admissible, and may be considered on any relevant matter).

    2. <u>When admissible</u>:

        a. In a civil case.

    and b. In which a claim for damages (or other relief) relies on a party's alleged commission of conduct.

    and c. That conduct constitutes an offense of sexual assault or child molestation.

(b) **Requirements for a party who intends to offer evidence under this rule**.

    1. <u>Requirement</u>: The party must disclose the evidence to the defendant, *including*:

        a. Statements of witnesses.

    or b. A summary of any testimony that is expected to be offered.

    2. <u>Time limit</u>: Disclosure must be made:

        a. At least <u>15 days</u> before the scheduled date of trial.

    or b. At such later time as the court may allow for *good cause*.

(c) This rule shall not be construed to limit the admission or consideration of evidence under any other rule.

# ARTICLE V
# PRIVILEGES

## Rule 501. General Rule

a. The following privileges are governed by common law as interpreted by U.S. courts *("in light of reason and experience")*:
   1. Privileges of a witness.
   2. Privileges of a person.
   3. Privileges of a government.
   4. Privileges of a state or political subdivision of a state.

b. <u>Applicable law</u>: Where state law applies to a claim or defense, state law shall determine what is privileged.

c. <u>Exception to applying common law</u>: A court should not look to state law privilege if otherwise required in:
   1. The U.S. Constitution.
   or 2. Act of Congress.
   or 3. The FRE.
   or 4. Other rules prescribed by the U.S. Supreme Court pursuant to statutory authority.

**Summary of Advisory Committee's Notes on Rule 501**
- Rule 501 provides that privileges shall continue to be developed by the courts of the United States under the standard of Rule 26 of the Federal Rules of Criminal Procedure, which requires that a federally developed common law based on modern reason and experience shall apply (in both civil and criminal cases) except where the state nature of the issues makes state privilege law the wiser course, as in the usual diversity case. Basically, federal law should not supersede state law in substantive areas such as privilege without a compelling reason.
- In federal question cases, federally evolved rules on privilege should apply since it is federal policy that is being enforced. On the other hand, in diversity cases where the case turns on a substantive question of state law and is brought in the federal courts because the parties reside in different states, the committee believes it is clear that state rules of privilege should apply unless the proof is directed at a claim or defense for which federal law supplies the rule of decision (a situation that would not commonly arise).
- The Committee believes that in civil cases in the federal courts, where an element of a claim or defense is not grounded upon a federal question, there is no federal interest strong enough to justify departure from state policy.
- In addition, the Committee seeks to avoid forum shopping in some civil actions, depending upon differences in the privilege law applied as among the state and federal courts.
- An additional note provided by the comments is that the prohibition against spouses testifying against each other is considered a rule of privilege (which is covered by this rule and not by Rule 601 (competency of witnesses)).

# ARTICLE VI
# WITNESSES

## Rule 601. General Rule of Competency

a. Except as otherwise provided by these rules, <u>every person is competent to be a witness</u>.

b. Where state law applies to a claim or defense, state law shall determine the competency of a witness.

---

**Summary of Advisory Committee's Notes on Rule 601**

- This rule eliminates all grounds of incompetency not specifically recognized in the succeeding rules of Article VI.
- The following are examples of grounds for incompetency that CANNOT be used to impeach a witness under Rule 601:
  - Religious belief.
  - Conviction of a crime.
  - Connection with the litigation as a party.
  - Connection to the litigation as an interested person or a spouse of an interested person.
- Note that Rule 601 does not specify any mental or moral qualifications for testifying as a witness. This is probably because standards of mental capacity have proved impractical in actual application.
- Discretion is regularly exercised in favor of *allowing* the testimony of a witness.
- The question of competency is one particularly suited for a jury to decide as one of weight and credibility (subject, of course, to judicial authority to review the fullness in terms of his own answers about it).
- <u>Moral qualifications</u>: Standards of moral qualifications consist essentially of evaluating a person's truthfulness in terms of her own answers about it. Their principal utility is in affording the opportunity to impress upon the witness her moral duty on *voir dire* examination. This result may be accomplished by administering an oath under Rule 603.
- <u>Religious beliefs</u>: Admissibility of religious belief as a ground to hold that a witness is incompetent to testify is treated in Rule 610.
- <u>Conviction of a crime</u>: Admissibility of a conviction to impeach a witness's testimony is dealt with in Rule 609.

---

## Rule 602. Lack of Personal Knowledge

a. A witness may testify to a matter only if there is <u>sufficient evidence</u> that the witness has *personal knowledge* of that matter (this evidence may include that witness's testimony).

b. This rule is subject to Rule 703 (optional testimony of an expert witness).

## Rule 603. Oath or Affirmation

a. Before testifying, every witness must take an oath or affirmation that the witness will testify truthfully.

b. **The oath or affirmation** must be given in a way that will:
    1. *"awaken the witness' conscience."*
and 2. *"impress the witness' mind"* with the duty to testify truthfully.

## Rule 604. Interpreters

An interpreter is subject to the rules on:

    1. Expert qualification.
and 2. Taking an oath to make a true translation.

# Rule 605. Competency of Judge as Witness

a. The trial judge may not testify as a witness.

b. <u>Automatic objection</u>: The opponent need not make an objection in order to enforce this (it is "automatic").

---

**Summary of Advisory Committee's Notes on Rule 605**

- 28 U.S.C. §455 requires that a judge disqualify himself in *"any case in which he * * * is or has been a material witness."* Even though the likelihood that the presiding judge in a federal court might be called to testify in the trial over which he is presiding is slight, the possibility is there.
- The solution here is a broad rule of incompetency, rather than incompetency only as to material matters. This leaves the matter to the discretion of the judge, or recognizing no incompetency. This was decided because of the inability to get satisfactory answers to questions that arise when the judge abandons the bench for the witness stand. Who rules on objections? Who compels her to answer? Can she rule impartially on the weight and admissibility of her own testimony? Can she be impeached or cross-examined effectively? Can she, in a jury trial, avoid conferring her seal of approval on one side in the eyes of the jury? Can she, in a bench trial, avoid an involvement destructive of impartiality?
- This rule provides an "automatic" objection. To require an actual objection would force the opponent to choose between not objecting, which would allow the testimony, and objecting, with the probable result of excluding the testimony but at the price of continuing the trial before a judge likely to feel that his integrity had been attacked by the objector.

---

# Rule 606. Competency of Juror as Witness

(a) **At the trial.**
1. A member of the trial jury may not testify as a witness before the jury of which he is a member.
2. The opponent may object <u>out of the jury's presence</u> if the juror is called to testify.

(b) **Inquiry into validity of verdict or indictment.**
1. When there is an inquiry into the validity of a <u>verdict</u> or <u>indict-ment,</u> a juror <u>may not</u> testify as to:
   a. Any matter or statement made <u>during jury deliberations</u>.
   or b. Anything of that juror's <u>thoughts or emotions</u> that caused the juror to agree/disagree with the verdict or indictment.
   or c. The juror's <u>mental processes</u> in connection with agreeing/ disagreeing with the verdict or indictment.
2. <u>Exception</u>: A juror may testify as to:
   1. Whether any extraneous prejudicial information was improperly brought to the jury's attention.
   or 2. Whether there was any outside influence on any juror.
   or 3. Whether there was a mistake in entering the verdict onto the verdict form.

3. This rule also applies to juror affidavits or other evidence of jurors' statements (involving the validity of a verdict or indictment).

---

**Summary of Advisory Committee's Notes on Rule 606**

- The considerations of this rule are similar to those of Rule 605, but without the need for an automatic objection; the only provision on objection is that opportunity be afforded for its making out of the presence of the jury.
- Subdivision (b) reflects the differences of opinion on whether testimony, affidavits, or statements of jurors should be received for the purpose of invalidating or supporting a verdict or indictment, and if so, under what circumstances. The values sought to be promoted by excluding the evidence include <u>freedom of deliberation</u>, stability and finality of verdicts, and <u>protection of jurors</u> against annoyance and embarrassment. (<u>McDonald v. Piess</u>, 238 U.S. 264 (1915)). On the other hand, simply putting verdicts beyond effective reach can only promote irregularity and injustice. The rule offers an accommodation between these competing considerations.
- This rule does not purport to specify the substantive grounds for setting aside verdicts for irregularity; it deals only with the competency of jurors to testify concerning those grounds. Allowing jurors to testify as to matters other than their own inner reactions involves no particular danger to the values sought to be protected.
- See also Rule 6(e) of the Federal Rules of Criminal Procedure and 18 U.S.C. §3500, governing the secrecy of grand jury proceedings. The present rule does not relate to secrecy and disclosure but to the competency of certain witnesses and evidence.

---

# Rule 607. Who May Impeach

Any party (including the party calling the witness) may attack the credibility of a witness.

---

**Summary of Advisory Committee's Notes on Rule 607**

- This rule abandons the traditional rule against impeaching one's own witness. A party rarely has a free choice in selecting his witnesses, and therefore does not hold them out as worthy of belief. To deny the right to impeach a witness would leave the party at the mercy of the witness and the adversary.
- Note that if the impeachment is by a prior statement, it is free from hearsay dangers and is excluded from Rule 801(d)(1). Revised Rule 32(a)(1) of the Federal Rules of Civil Procedure allows any party to impeach a witness by means of his deposition, and Rule 43(b) has allowed the calling and impeachment of an adverse party or person identified with him.

# Rule 608. Evidence of Character and Conduct of Witness

**(a) Opinion and reputation evidence of character.**

    (1) When dealing with the **character** of the witness, opinion or reputation evidence will be limited to <u>truthfulness</u> or <u>untruthfulness</u>.

    (2) Evidence of <u>truthful character</u> is admissible only after the witness's character of truthfulness has been attacked (by opinion or reputation testimony or otherwise).

**(b) Specific instances of conduct.**

    1. Specific instances of a witness's conduct that are used to support or attack a witness's "character for truthfulness" can be proved only by what the witness says in cross-examination, and not outside evidence.

    2. <u>Requirements</u>:

        a. The "instances" have to be probative of *truthfulness or untruthfulness.*

        b. The <u>cross-examination</u> must concern:

            (1) The witness's character for truthfulness.

        or  (2) The character for truthfulness of another witness as to whom the witness testified.

    3. <u>Exception to 608(b)</u>: Conviction of a crime may be proved by extrinsic evidence (see Rule 609).

    4. The court has discretion whether or not to allow cross-examination.

    5. A witness testifying <u>does not</u> waive the privilege against self-incrimination as to questions that bear <u>only</u> on his character for truthfulness.

---

**Summary of Advisory Committee's Notes on Rule 608**

- Rule 404(a) provides that character evidence is not admissible for the purpose of proving that the person acted in conformity with that character.
  - This rule is subject to several exceptions, one of which is character evidence of a witness as bearing upon her character for truthfulness. This rule develops that exception.
  - The rule is strictly limited to character for veracity, rather than allowing evidence as to character generally. This is meant to <u>sharpen relevancy</u>; to <u>reduce surprise</u>, <u>waste of time</u>, and <u>confusion</u>; and to make the lot of the witness somewhat less unattractive.
  - The use of opinion and reputation evidence as means of proving the character of witnesses is consistent with Rule 405(a). While modern practice has purported to exclude opinion witnesses who testify to reputation, witnesses seem in fact often to be giving their opinions, disguised somewhat misleadingly as reputation. And even under the modern practice, a common relaxation has

allowed inquiry as to whether the witnesses would believe the principal witness under oath.

- Character evidence in support of character for truthfulness is admissible under the rule only after the witness's character has first been attacked, as has been the case at common law. Another practice would waste too much time.
- Opinion or reputation that the witness is untruthful specifically qualifies as an attack under the rule, and evidence of misconduct, including conviction of crime and of corruption, also fall within this category. Evidence of bias or interest does not.

- Subdivision (b) is in conformity with Rule 405 and bars evidence of specific instances of conduct of a witness for the purpose of attacking or supporting his character for truthfulness. There are, however, two exceptions:

    **(1)** Specific instances are provable when they have been the subject of criminal conviction (conviction of crime as a technique of impeachment is treated in detail in Rule 609).

    and **(2)** Specific instances may be inquired into on cross-examination of the principal witness or of a witness giving an opinion of his character for truthfulness.

- Effective cross-examination demands that some allowance be made for going into matters of this kind, but there are substantial possibilities of abuse. Therefore, specific requirements are set: The instances inquired into must be probative of truthfulness or its opposite and not remote in time. Also, the overriding protection of Rule 403 requires that probative value not be outweighed by danger of unfair prejudice, confusion of issues, or misleading the jury, and that of Rule 611 bars harassment and undue embarrassment.
- The final sentence makes clear that in light of the privilege against self-incrimination, not every past criminal act relevant to character for truthfulness may be inquired into on cross-examination. To hold this would reduce the privilege to a nullity. While it is true that an accused, unlike an ordinary witness, has an option whether to testify (if the option meant opening up inquiry as to any and all criminal acts committed during a witness's lifetime), the right to testify would barely have much meaning.

# Rule 609. Impeachment by Evidence of Conviction of Crime

(a) **General rule**.

    (1) <u>Admissibility of evidence attacking the truthfulness of a witness</u>:

        a. <u>Witness other than an accused</u>: Evidence that a witness has been convicted of a crime is <u>admissible</u> (subject to Rule 403) *only* if:

            1. The crime is punishable by death.

        or  2. The crime is punishable by more than one year in prison.

        b. <u>Accused as witness</u>: Evidence that the accused has been convicted of a crime is <u>admissible</u> if its "probative value outweighs its prejudicial effect to the accused" (court has discretion).

(2) If the elements of a crime (regardless of punishment) require proof (or admission, in the case of a guilty plea) of an act of <u>dishonesty</u> or a <u>false statement</u> by a witness, evidence as to that crime is <u>admissible</u> against any witness.

(b) **Time limit.**

1. Evidence of a conviction is admissible only until <u>the *later* of</u>:
    a. <u>10 years</u> after the conviction date.
    or b. <u>10 years</u> after the release of the witness from prison (for the conviction in the testimony).

2. <u>Exception to 10-year time limit</u>: Evidence of a witness's conviction will be admitted after 10 years if:
    a. The court determines *"in the interests of justice"* that "the probative value of the conviction supported by specific facts and circumstances *substantially outweighs* its prejudicial effect."
    and b. <u>Notice is given</u>: The party using the evidence gives the adverse party notice of intent to use the evidence:
        1. In advance.
        and 2. In writing.

3. <u>Purpose</u>: To allow the adverse party to contest the use of the evidence.

(c) **Effect of pardon, annulment, or certificate of rehabilitation.**

<u>Evidence of a conviction is inadmissible if</u>:

(1) **Effect of rehabilitation —**
    a. The conviction was the subject of:
        1. A pardon.
        or 2. An annulment.
        or 3. A certificate of rehabilitation.
        or 4. Any other procedure based on the rehabilitation of the convict.
    and b. The convict <u>was not</u> convicted of a later crime that was:
        1. Punishable by death.
        or 2. Punishable by more than one year in prison.

or (2) **Effect of finding of innocence —** The conviction was the subject of:
    a. A pardon.
    or b. An annulment
    or c. Any other procedure based on a finding of innocence.

(d) **Juvenile adjudications.**

Evidence of juvenile adjudications is <u>admissible</u> only if:

1. The case is a criminal case.
and 2. The witness is someone other than the accused.

and 3. Conviction of the event would be admissible against the credibility of an adult.

and 4. The court believes that admission is <u>necessary</u> to fairly determine guilt or innocence.

(e) **Pendency of appeal.**

1. <u>Effect on admissibility of a conviction</u>: The pendency of an appeal does not render evidence of a conviction inadmissible.

2. <u>Admissibility of the pendency itself</u>: Evidence of the pendency of an appeal is admissible.

---

**Summary of Advisory Committee's Notes on Rule 609**

- <u>Evidence of a conviction of a crime</u> is significant only as a method to impeach a witness because it stands as proof of the commission of the underlying criminal act.
- The weight of traditional authority has been to generally allow the use of felonies (without regard to the nature of the particular offense and of *crimen falsi* without regard to the grade of the offense).
- Subdivision (a) divides crimes into two categories:
  - Subdivision (a)(1) includes crimes regarded as a felony-grade crime (without regard to the nature of the defense).
  - Subdivision (a)(2) involves dishonest or false statements (without regard to the grade of the offense).
- Provable convictions are not limited to violations of federal law.
- The 2006 amendment provides that evidence of a conviction is mandated only when the conviction required the proof (or admission, in the case of a guilty plea) of an act of dishonesty or false statement. Evidence of all other convictions is inadmissible under this subsection, whether or not the witness was dishonest or made a false statement in the process of the crime (e.g., evidence that a witness was convicted for a crime of violence, such as murder, is not admissible under Rule 609(a)(2), even if the witness acted deceitfully in the course of committing the crime).

---

# Rule 610. Religious Beliefs or Opinions

A witness's beliefs or opinions on <u>religious matters</u> are not admissible to weaken or strengthen the witness's credibility.

---

**Summary of Advisory Committee's Notes on Rule 610**

While this rule prohibits inquiry into the religious beliefs or opinions of a witness for the purpose of showing that her character for truthfulness is affected by their nature, an inquiry for the purpose of showing interest or bias because of them is not within the prohibition (e.g., disclosure of affiliation with a church that is a party to the litigation would be allowable under the rule).

# Rule 611. Mode and Order of Interrogation and Presentation

(a) **Control by court.**
  1. The court shall *reasonably control* the mode and order of:
      a. Interrogating witnesses.
    and b. Presenting evidence.
  2. <u>Purpose</u>:
      (1) To make the interrogation/presentation effective in ascertaining the truth.
    and (2) To avoid waste of time.
    and (3) To protect witnesses from harassment or undue embarrassment.

(b) **Scope of cross-examination.**
  1. Cross-examination should be limited to:
      a. The subject matter of the direct examination.
      b. Matters affecting the credibility of the witness.
  2. The court has discretion to allow questioning on other matters.

(c) **Leading questions.**
  1. <u>Direct examination</u>: Leading questions may be used only if:
      a. They are needed to develop the witness's testimony.
    or b. A party calls *either:*
        i. A hostile witness.
      or ii. An adverse party.
      or iii. A witness identified with an adverse party.
  2. <u>Cross-examination</u>: Ordinarily, leading questions are permitted.

---

**Summary of Advisory Committee's Notes on Rule 611**
- It is not feasible to spell out detailed rules to govern the mode and order of interrogating witnesses presenting evidence. The ultimate responsibility for the effective working of the adversary system rests with the judge.
- The rule sets forth the objectives the judge should seek to attain.
  (1) Concerns such as <u>whether testimony should be in the form of a free narrative</u> or <u>responses to specific questions</u>, the <u>order of calling witnesses and presenting evidence</u>, the <u>use of demonstrative evidence</u>, and the many other questions arising during the course of a trial can be solved only by the judge's common sense and fairness in view of the particular circumstances.
  (2) <u>Avoidance of needless consumption of time</u>. A similar rule is Rule 403(b).
  (3) <u>Whether interrogation tactics entail harassment or undue embarrassment</u>. Pertinent circumstances include the importance of the testimony, the nature of the inquiry, its relevance to credibility, waste of time, and confusion.
- Subdivision (b) reflects the tradition in the federal courts and in many state courts to limit the scope of cross-examination to matters testified to on direct and matters bearing upon the credibility of the witness. Various reasons have been given for this:

(1) A party vouches for her own witness but only to the extent of matters asked about on direct.

(2) A party may not ask his own witness leading questions (although this may not be necessary for a proper development of the testimony).

(3) A practice of limited cross-examination promotes orderly presentation of the case. While this third reason has merit, it essentially deals with the order of presentation and not one in which involvement at the appellate level is likely to be useful.

- Subdivision (c) continues the traditional view that the suggestive powers of the leading question are undesirable. However, numerous exceptions have achieved recognition: The witness who is hostile, unwilling, or biased; the child witness or the adult with communication problems; the witness whose recollection is exhausted; and undisputed preliminary matters.

- Appellate courts will almost never reverse for infractions. The matter clearly falls within the area of control by the judge over the mode and order of interrogation and presentation and accordingly is phrased in words of suggestion rather than command.

- The rule also conforms to allow the use of leading questions on cross-examination.

- The purpose of the term "*ordinarily*" is to allow judges to deny the use of leading questions when the cross-examination is cross-examination *in form only* and not in fact (as for example the "cross-examination" of a party by his own counsel after being called by the opponent (savoring more of re-direct) or of an insured defendant who proves to be friendly to the plaintiff).

- The final sentence deals with witnesses who are automatically regarded and treated as hostile. Rule 43(b) of the Federal Rules of Civil Procedure has included only "*an adverse party or an officer, director, or managing agent of a public or private corporation or of a partnership or association which is an adverse party.*" This limitation to persons whose statements would stand as admissions is believed to be an unduly narrow concept of those who may safely be regarded as hostile without further demonstration.

# Rule 612. Writing Used to Refresh Memory

a. A witness may use a writing to refresh her memory:
    (1) While testifying.
or (2) Before testifying.

b. <u>Adverse party's rights</u>:
    i. For writings used under (1) above, the adverse party may:
        1. Have the writing produced at the hearing.
    or 2. Inspect the writing.
    or 3. Cross-examine the witness on the writing.
    or 4. Introduce relevant portions as evidence.
    ii. Under (2), these are in the court's discretion.

c. <u>If writing is claimed to be irrelevant to testimony</u>:
    1. The court will examine and cut out any such parts of the writing.
    2. The parts that were cut out will be saved for the appellate court in the event of an appeal.

d. <u>If writing not produced</u>:
    1. **Noncriminal cases**: The court can make any order that *justice requires*.
    2. **Criminal cases** (where prosecution does not comply): The court can *either*:
        a. Strike the testimony.
    or  b. Declare a mistrial, if the court in its discretion determines that *"the interests of justice so require."*

e. This rule is subject to the provisions of 18 U.S.C. §3500.

---

**Summary of Advisory Committee's Notes on Rule 612**

- Rule 612 provides that (except as set forth in 18 U.S.C. §3500), if a witness uses a writing to refresh his memory while testifying (and for the purpose of testifying), an adverse party is entitled to have the writing <u>produced at the hearing</u>, <u>to inspect it</u>, <u>to cross-examine the witness on it</u>, and to <u>introduce in evidence</u> those portions relating to the witness's testimony.

- The production of writings used by a witness to refresh his memory before testifying is <u>discretionary</u>. (See <u>Goldman v. United States</u>, 316 U.S. 129 (1942)). The Committee thought that allowing an adverse party to require the production of writings used before testifying could result in fishing expeditions among the many papers a witness may have used in preparing for trial. Nothing in this rule should be construed as barring a privilege with respect to writings used by a witness to refresh his memory.

- The purpose of the phrase "for the purpose of testifying" is to safeguard against using the rule as a pretext for a complete search of an opposing party's files. It ensures that access is limited only to those writings that may fairly be said to have an impact upon the testimony of the witness. This is in keeping with the purpose of the rule to promote the search of credibility and memory.

---

# Rule 613. Prior Statements of Witnesses

(a) **Examining witness concerning prior statement.**
    1. When questioning a witness about a prior statement (written or not), the attorney does not have to show or disclose the contents of that prior statement to the witness.
    2. On request, the attorney has to show or disclose the contents of the statement to opposing counsel.

(b) **Extrinsic evidence of prior inconsistent statement of witness.**
    1. Extrinsic evidence of a prior inconsistent statement is admissible only if:
        a. *Both*:
            i.  The witness is given a chance to explain/deny the evidence.
          and ii.  The opposite party is given a chance to interrogate the witness on the evidence.
        or  b. *The interests of justice otherwise require.*
    2. This does not apply to 801(d)(2) admissions (admissions of a party-opponent).

**Summary of Advisory Committee's Notes on Rule 613**
- Subdivision (a) abolishes the useless impediment that a cross-examiner, prior to questioning the witness about her own prior statement in writing, must first show it to the witness. The provision for disclosure to counsel is to protect against unwarranted insinuations that a statement has been made when the fact is to the contrary.
  - The rule does not defeat Rule 1002, which relates to production of an original when the contents of a writing are sought to be proved.
  - This rule also does not defeat Rule 26(b)(3) of the Rules of Civil Procedure, entitling a person on request to a copy of his own statement, though the operation of the latter may be suspended temporarily.
- The requirement that an impeaching statement first be shown to the witness before it can be proved by extrinsic evidence is preserved but with some modifications in subdivision (b).
  - The witness must simply be given the opportunity to explain and the opposite party must be given an opportunity to examine the statement, with no specification of any particular time or sequence.
  - A measure of discretion is given to the judge to allow for such things as the witness becoming unavailable by the time the statement is discovered.

# Rule 614. Calling and Interrogation of Witnesses by Court

(a) **Calling by court.**
>   1. The court may call witnesses:
>       a. At its own discretion.
>   or  b. At the suggestion of a party.
>   2. All parties may cross examine any witness called.

(b) **Interrogation by court.**
> The court may interrogate witnesses (whether they were called by the court or called by a party).

(c) **Objections.**
> Objections to (a) or (b) may be made when the jury is not present (be it at the time the calling/interrogation is made or at the next available opportunity).

**Summary of Advisory Committee's Notes on Rule 614**
- The authority of the judge to **call** witnesses is well established.
- Some of the reasons are to assure the right to cross-examine effectively, to avoid the tendency of juries to associate a witness with the party calling him (regardless of technical aspects of vouching), and to free the judge from the case as made by the parties.
- The authority of the judge to **question** witnesses is also well established. This does not mean that a judge may assume the role of advocate, although the exact

manner in which interrogation should be conducted (and the proper extent of it) cannot be put in a rule.

- The provision relating to <u>objections</u> is here to relieve counsel of the embarrassment of objecting to the judge's questions in the jury's presence, while at the same time assuring that objections are made with enough time to give the opportunity to take possible corrective measures.

## Rule 615. Exclusion of Witnesses

a. The court shall order witnesses not to hear other witnesses' testimony (i.e., to be excluded) *either*:
    1. At the request of a party.
or  2. On its own motion.

b. The following <u>may not</u> be excluded:
    (1) A **party** to the action.
    (2) A **representative** (officer or employee designated by attorney) of a party that is <u>not</u> a natural person.
    (3) A person whose **presence is** *essential* to the presentation of a party's cause, as shown by that party.
    (4) A person authorized by statute.

### Summary of Advisory Committee's Notes on Rule 615

- <u>Excluding or sequestering witnesses</u> has long been recognized as a means of discouraging and exposing <u>fabrication</u>, <u>inaccuracy</u>, and <u>collusion</u>.
- The rule takes the position that the matter is one of *<u>right</u>*, and not one of discretion.
- No time is specified for making the request to exclude or sequester a witness.
- **<u>The following are not subject to exclusion</u>:**
    (1) <u>Persons who are parties,</u> as this would raise serious problems of confrontation and due process.
    (2) <u>A party who is not a natural person</u> is entitled to have a representative present. This is the equivalent of the right of a natural-person party to be present. Most cases involve allowing a police officer in charge of an investigation to remain in court despite the fact that she will be a witness. The attorney, not the client, designates the representative. This is the simplest way to work the rule and it is assumed that the attorney will follow the client's wishes.
    (3) <u>An agent who handled the transaction being litigated</u> or <u>an expert</u> needed to advise counsel in the management of the litigation.

# ARTICLE VII
# OPINIONS AND EXPERT TESTIMONY

## Rule 701. Opinion Testimony by Lay Witnesses

If the witness is <u>not</u> testifying as an expert, the only **opinions** or **inferences** allowed are those:

(a) *Rationally based on the perception of the witness.*

(b) Helpful for:
    1. A clear understanding of the witness's testimony.
or   2. Determining a fact in issue.

and (c) <u>NOT</u> based on <u>scientific</u>, <u>technical</u>, or <u>other specialized knowledge</u> that falls within the scope of Rule 702 ("Testimony by Experts").

---

**Summary of Advisory Committee's Notes on Rule 701**
- This rule's objective is to provide the trier of fact with an *accurate reproduction of the event*.
- The two limitations are that there must be:
    **(1)** Firsthand knowledge or observation.
  and **(2)** The testimony has to be helpful in resolving issues.
- Other standards are too difficult to administer.
  - It is too hard for witnesses to express themselves in language that is not that of an opinion or conclusion, and imposing a *"necessity"* standard would be too hard to enforce.
  - Also, it is almost impossible to determine by rule what is a "fact."
- The rule assumes that the natural course of direct and cross-examination will be effective in showing both parties' strengths and weaknesses.
- An amendment on December 1, 2000, adding subparagraph (c) was made to prevent a party from offering an expert witness as a lay witness ("hiding an expert witness in lay witness clothing") and thereby evading the requirements of Rule 702, as well as the requirements of the Federal Rules of Civil Procedure and Federal Rules of Criminal Procedure to disclose expert witness information. All testimony that is actually expert testimony is now channeled to Rule 702.

---

## Rule 702. Testimony by Experts

a. An expert's **opinion** (or other form of testimony) may be used to provide **scientific, technical,** or **other specialized knowledge,** if it is helpful for *either*:
    1. Understanding the evidence.
    2. Determining a fact in issue.

b. An **"expert"** is someone who is qualified by:
    1. Knowledge.
or   2. Skill.

or 3. Experience.
or 4. Training.
or 5. Education.

c. Reliability:
The expert testimony will be admissible only if:
(1) The testimony is based upon sufficient facts or data.
and (2) The testimony is the product of reliable principles and methods.
and (3) The witness has applied the principles and methods reliably to the facts of the case.

---

**Summary of Advisory Committee's Notes on Rule 702**

- It is too difficult to evaluate facts without applying some scientific, technical, or other specialized knowledge. The most common source of this knowledge is the expert witness, although there are other techniques.
- The rule recognizes that an expert does not always give an opinion on the case. He may give scientific or other principles relevant to the case, leaving the trier of fact to apply them to the facts. The use of opinions is permissible only for certain purposes (See Rules 703 to 705).
- Whether or not a situation calls for the use of expert testimony depends on *whether a lay person can determine the particular issue at hand without the use of an expert*.
- The fields of knowledge are not limited to "scientific" and "technical" but extend to all "*specialized*" knowledge. Also, the notion of "expert" is viewed in a broad sense. So, for purposes of the rule, experts are not only such in the strictest sense of the word (e.g., physicians, physicists, and architects), but they also consist of a large group sometimes called "*skilled*" witnesses (e.g., bankers or landowners testifying to land values).
- The amendment on December 1, 2000, adding the requirement of "reliability" emphasizes that the court is the "gatekeeper" responsible for keeping out unreliable expert testimony. The amendment provides the court with general standards to assess the reliability and helpfulness of the testimony being offered.

---

# Rule 703. Bases of Opinion Testimony by Experts

a. An expert can base **opinions** and **inferences** on facts/data that:
1. The expert perceives.
2. The expert is informed of at or before the hearing.

b. If experts in the field *reasonably rely* on the same type of facts or data (as in the case) when they form their opinions, the facts or data do not have to be admissible as evidence.

c. Facts or data that are otherwise inadmissible (see b.) may not be disclosed to the jury by the expert or by inference, <u>unless</u> the court determines that the probative value (in helping the jury evaluate the expert's opinion) *substantially outweighs* the prejudicial effect.

**Summary of Advisory Committee's Notes on Rule 703**

- Facts or data upon which expert opinions are based may come from three possible sources:
  (1) <u>The witness's firsthand observation</u> (e.g., a treating physician). (See Rule 705 for whether she must first relate her observations.)
  (2) <u>Presentation at the trial</u>. This may be by asking the expert a hypothetical question or by having the expert attend the trial and hear the testimony establishing the facts (Rule 705 is used to determine what testimony the expert relied upon).
  (3) <u>Presentation of data to the expert otherwise</u>.
- This broadens the basis for expert opinions. As an example, a physician in his own practice bases his diagnosis on information from many sources, including (a) statements by patients and relatives, (b) reports and opinions from nurses, technicians, and other doctors, (c) hospital records, and (d) X-rays. A physician relies upon these in making life-and-death decisions. His validation, expertly performed and subject to cross-examination, is enough to allow the above as evidence.

## Rule 704. Opinion on Ultimate Issue

(a) Normally, **opinion testimony** is not open to objection just because it *embraces an "ultimate issue"* to be decided by the trier of fact.

(b) <u>Mental state exception</u>: An expert's **opinion testimony** may not be used to show that an accused had a particular mental state or condition that constitutes an element of a crime or a defense. (The trier of fact must determine this on its own.)

**Summary of Advisory Committee's Notes on Rule 704**

- The basic approach to opinions (both lay and expert) is to admit them when they are helpful to the trier of fact.
- Older cases often contained rules against allowing witnesses to express opinions *upon ultimate issues*. This rule was unduly restrictive and difficult to apply. Witnesses could offer opinions without specifically violating the rule. This rule abolishes the "ultimate issue" rule.
- The rule does not allow for the admission of all opinions, however. Under Rules 701 and 702, opinions "*must be helpful to the trier of fact*," and Rule 403 excludes evidence that "*wastes time.*"
- These provisions assure that opinions that would tell the jury what result they should reach will not be admitted.
- They also exclude opinions phrased in terms of inadequately explored legal criteria (e.g., The question, "Did T have capacity to make a will?" would be excluded, while the question, "Did T have sufficient mental capacity to know the nature and extent of his property and the natural objects of his bounty and to formulate a rational scheme of distribution?" would be allowed).

## Rule 705. Disclosure of Facts or Data Underlying Expert Opinion

a. An expert witness does not have to testify about the facts or data that underlie her **opinion** or **inference**.

b. Exceptions: The expert must testify about underlying facts if:
    1. The court requires it.
    2. The expert is asked to disclose the facts on cross-examination.

---

**Summary of Advisory Committee's Notes on Rule 705**

- This rule eliminates the requirement of preliminary disclosure of underlying facts or data at the trial. It allows counsel, however, to make disclosure of the underlying facts or data as a preliminary to the giving of an expert opinion, if he chooses.
- This is similar to Rule 4515 of the New York Civil Practice Law and Rules, which states that *"unless the court orders otherwise, questions calling for the opinion of an expert witness need not be hypothetical in form, and the witness may state his opinion and reasons without first specifying the data upon which it is based. Upon cross-examination, he may be required to specify the data . . ."*

---

## Rule 706. Court Appointed Experts

(a) **Appointment.**
    1. A court may enter an order to show cause explaining why an expert witness should not be appointed:
        a. On its own motion.
    or  b. On the motion of any party.
    2. The court may request the parties to submit nominations (for potential experts).
    3. The court may appoint expert witnesses that are either:
        a. Agreed upon by the parties.
    or  b. Selected by the court.
    4. Requirements for an appointed expert witness:
        a. The expert **must consent** to act.
    and b. The court **must inform** the expert of his duties either:
            i.  In writing (a copy must be filed with the clerk).
        or  ii. At a conference where the parties can participate.
    and c. The expert witness **must advise** the parties of his findings.
    5. Rights of the parties:
        a. The witness's deposition may be taken by any party.
        b. The witness may be called to testify by the court or any party.
        c. The witness may be cross-examined by any party.

(b) **Compensation.**
    1. Amount: A *reasonable sum* allowed by the court.
    2. Source of funds:
        a. Criminal and civil "just compensation" cases: Government usually pays.

     b. <u>Other civil cases</u>:
          i.  The parties pay according to the court's apportioning.
         ii.  The costs are then charged just like any other court costs.

**(c) Disclosure of appointment.**

The court has *discretion* to decide whether or not to tell the jury that the expert has been appointed.

**(d) Parties' experts of own selection.**

Parties may call their own experts.

---

**Summary of Advisory Committee's Notes on Rule 706**

- There is an increasing trend to provide for the use of court-appointed experts.
- This shows concern for matters such as shopping for experts, the corruption of some experts, and the reluctance of many reputable experts to involve themselves in litigation.
- Actual appointment does not happen frequently, but one can assume that the availability of the procedure in itself decreases the need for using it. The possibility that the judge may appoint an expert in a given case must have some effect on the expert witness of a party and upon the person utilizing her services.
- In the federal practice, a comprehensive scheme for court-appointed experts was initiated with the adoption of Rule 28 of the Federal Rules of Criminal Procedure in 1946. Rule 706, using much of the same language, expands the practice to include civil cases.

# ARTICLE VIII
# HEARSAY

## INTRODUCTORY NOTE: THE HEARSAY PROBLEM

- In evaluating the testimony of a witness, <u>perception</u>, <u>memory</u>, and <u>narration</u> are all factors that are considered. So that the witness does his best with respect to each of these factors, and so that any inaccuracies are exposed, there <u>are three conditions under which witnesses will ideally be required to testify</u>:
    (1) <u>Under oath</u>. Standard procedure calls for the swearing of witnesses. The requirement is relaxed only to allow affirmation by persons with scruples against taking oaths.
    (2) <u>In the personal presence of the trier of fact</u>. The demeanor of the witness is believed to give the parties valuable clues. A witness may be less willing to lie in the presence of the person against whom her testimony is directed. Also, the witness will probably want to avoid public disgrace by being exposed as a liar.
    (3) <u>Subject to cross-examination</u>. There is a belief, or perhaps hope, that cross-examination is effective in exposing imperfections of perception, memory, and narration.
- Common sense tells us that most of the evidence that is not given under these three conditions may be better than evidence that is. And it is almost always better than no evidence at all. The problem is in balancing this idea with that of having the ideal conditions for testifying.
- Since no one advocates excluding all hearsay, there are three possible solutions:
    (1) <u>Admit all hearsay</u>. Abolition of the hearsay rule would be the simplest solution and would abolish the necessity of giving testimony under ideal conditions.
    (2) <u>Admit hearsay that has sufficient probative force, but with procedural safeguards</u>. Admissibility could be determined by weighing the probative force of the evidence against the possibility of prejudice, waste of time, and the availability of more satisfactory evidence. Procedural safeguards could be notice of intention to use hearsay, free comment by the judge on the weight of the evidence, and a greater measure of authority in both trial and appellate judges to deal with evidence on the basis of weight. The problems with this approach are the amount of judicial discretion, the minimized predictability of rulings, the enhanced difficulties of preparing for trial, the added element to the already

overcomplicated pretrial procedures, and the requirement of substantially different rules for civil and criminal cases.

(3) <u>Revise the present system of class exceptions</u>. The approach to hearsay in these rules is a general rule excluding hearsay, with exceptions. The hearsay exceptions are collected under two rules, one dealing with situations where availability of the declarant is immaterial (Rule 803) and the other dealing with those where unavailability is made a condition to the admission of the hearsay statement (Rule 804). This plan has been criticized for being bulky and complex, failing to screen good from bad hearsay realistically, and inhibiting the growth of the law of evidence.

- The rules have been calculated to encourage growth and development in this area of the law, while conserving the values and experience of the past as a guide to the future.

## Rule 801. Definitions

(a) **"Statement"** includes:

(1) An oral or written assertion.

or (2) Conduct (nonverbal) of a person, if that person intended it to be an assertion.

(b) **"Declarant."**

A person who makes a statement.

(c) **"Hearsay."**

1. A statement offered in evidence to prove that what the statement asserts is true.

2. Made by the declarant while not testifying.

(d) **Statements which are not hearsay.**

(1) **Prior statement by witness**: A prior statement of a witness is <u>not</u> hearsay if:

    i. The declarant testifies and is subject to cross-examination on the statement.

and ii. <u>The statement is either</u>:

    (A) Inconsistent with the testimony <u>and</u> was given under oath (at a trial, hearing, other proceeding, or deposition).

or (B) Consistent with the testimony <u>and</u> is offered to dispute a charge (express or implied) that the declarant

    1. Lied.

or 2. Was subject to improper influence.

or 3. Had an improper motive.

or (C) A statement that identifies a person who was seen (or heard).

(2) **Admission by party-opponent**.
1. A statement that is offered against a party is <u>not</u> hearsay if:
    (A) The statement is the **party's own statement** (as an individual or as a representative).
  or (B) The party seems to have **adopted or believed** the statement to be true.
  or (C) The person making the statement was **autho-rized** by the party to speak.
  or (D) The statement was:
        1. Made by an **agent** or **servant.**
    and 2. Made <u>during the existence</u> of the relation-ship.
    and 3. Concerning an issue <u>within the scope</u> of the relationship.
  or (E) The statement was made by a **co-conspirator** during and in advancement of the conspiracy.
2. The <u>contents</u> of the statement will be considered, but that is <u>not</u> enough in itself to establish any of the following:
    a. The <u>declarant's authority</u> under (C).
    b. The <u>agency or employment relationship</u> (and its scope) under (D).
    c. The <u>existence of a conspiracy</u> and the declarant's participation with the party against whom the statement is offered under (E).

**Summary of Advisory Committee's Notes on Rule 801**
- The definition of **"statement"** in subdivision (a) is important because the term is used in the definition of hearsay in subdivision (c). The effect is to exclude all evidence of conduct from the operation of the hearsay rule, including verbal or nonverbal evidence that is not intended as an assertion. The key to the definition is that nothing is an assertion unless intended to be one.
  - **Verbal assertions** fall into the category of "statement," since an assertion made in words is intended by the declarant to be an assertion.
  - Some **nonverbal conduct**, such as the act of pointing to identify a suspect in a lineup, is clearly the same as words and is to be regarded as a statement.
- All evidence comes with the possibility of fabrication, but it is less likely with nonverbal than with assertive verbal conduct.
- <u>Motivation</u>, the <u>nature of the conduct</u>, and the <u>presence or absence of reliance</u> will be important in determining the weight to be given the evidence.
- Verbal conduct that is *assertive* but offered as a basis for inferring something other than the matter asserted, is excluded from the definition of hearsay by the language of subdivision (c).
- When evidence of conduct is offered on the theory that it is not hearsay because it is not a statement, a preliminary determination will be required to determine whether an assertion is intended. The rule places the burden upon the party

claiming that the intention existed; ambiguous and doubtful cases will be resolved in favor of admissibility.

- In subdivision (d), several types of statements that would otherwise fall within the definition of hearsay are expressly excluded from it:

    (1) **Prior statement by witness.** A problem arises when the witness on the stand denies having made the statement or admits having made it but denies its truth. These statements are treated as hearsay because the conditions of oath, cross-examination, and demeanor observation were not effective at the time the statement was made and cannot adequately be supplied by the later examination. The rule requires that the declarant actually testify as a witness, and it then gives three situations in which the statement is excepted from the category of hearsay:

        (a) Prior inconsistent statements are substantive evidence. The statement must be inconsistent with the testimony given in order to assure that both versions are examined while the witness is on the stand.

        (b) Prior consistent statements are substantive evidence.

        (c) Prior identifications are substantive evidence. The basis for this exception is the inconclusive nature of courtroom identifications as compared with those made at an earlier time under less suggestive conditions.

    (2) **Admissions.** Admissions by a party-opponent are excluded from the category of hearsay on the theory that their admissibility in evidence is the result of the adversary system rather than satisfaction of the conditions of the hearsay rule. The rule specifies five categories of statements for which the *responsibility of a party* is enough to justify it being admitted into evidence against him:

        (a) A party's own statement is the classic example of an admission. If he is a representative and the statement is offered against him in that capacity, there is no requirement for an inquiry whether he was acting in the representative capacity in making the statement; the statement only has to be relevant to the issue at hand.

        (b) An admission made by adopting the statement of another. While knowledge of contents is normally essential, this is not always the case: "X is a reliable person and knows what he is talking about." Adoption may be shown in any appropriate manner. When silence is relied upon, the theory is that the person would protest the statement made in his presence if the statement were untrue.

        (c) A statement authorized by a party to be made should be considered an admission by the party. The rule is phrased broadly so as to encompass both statements to third persons and statements by the agent to the principal. A party's books or records are usable against her, without regard to any intent to disclose to third persons.

        (d) For the admissibility of statements by agents as admissions, we apply the usual test of agency, whether the admission was made by the agent acting in the scope of his employment.

        (e) The admissibility of statements of co-conspirators is limited to those statements made "during the course and in furtherance of the conspiracy."

## Rule 802. Hearsay Rule

a. **HEARSAY IS <u>INADMISSIBLE</u>.**

b. <u>Exceptions</u>: Hearsay is <u>admissible</u> where provided for by:
    1. The FRE.
or 2. Other rules prescribed by the U.S. Supreme Court pursuant to statutory authority.

---

**Summary of Advisory Committee's Notes on Rule 802**

- Hearsay that is made admissible by other rules adopted by the Supreme Court or by act of Congress is excepted from the operation of these rules. <u>Examples of the exceptions include</u>:
  - *Federal Rules of Civil Procedure*:
    - Rule 4(g): Proof of service by affidavit.
    - Rule 32: Admissibility of depositions.
    - Rule 43(e): Affidavits when motion based on facts not appearing of record.
    - Rule 56: Affidavits in summary judgment proceedings.
    - Rule 65(b): Showing by affidavit for temporary restraining order.
  - *Federal Rules of Criminal Procedure*:
    - Rule 4(a): Affidavits to show grounds for issuing warrants.
    - Rule 12(b)(4): Affidavits to determine issues of fact in connection with motions.

---

## Rule 803. Hearsay Exceptions; Availability of Declarant Immaterial

**THE HEARSAY RULE <u>DOES NOT</u> APPLY TO THE FOLLOWING (EVEN THOUGH THE DECLARANT IS AVAILABLE AS A WITNESS):**

(1) **Present sense impression.**
    This is a statement:
        a. Describing or explaining an event/condition.
    and b. Made **while** or **immediately after** the declarant was experiencing the event/condition.

(2) **Excited utterance.**
    This is a statement:
        a. About a *startling* event/condition.
    and b. Made while the declarant was under the stress of excitement caused by the event/condition.

(3) **Then existing mental, emotional, or physical condition.**
        a. These are statements of the declarant's then existing (at time statement made):
            1. State of mind.
            2. Emotion.
            3. Sensation.

  4. Physical condition.
  5. <u>Examples</u>: Intent, plan, motive, design, mental feeling, pain, bodily health.
 b. This does not include statements of memory (to prove the fact remembered) or belief (to prove the fact believed) unless the statement is about the <u>declarant's will</u>.

**(4) Statements for purposes of medical diagnosis or treatment.**
These are statements:
  a. Made for purposes of medical diagnosis or treatment.
and b. Describing any of the following (as long as they are reasonably related to the diagnosis or treatment):
   1. Medical history.
or 2. Past or present symptoms, pain, or sensations.
or 3. The general character of the cause of them.

**(5) Recorded recollection.**
  a. This is a memorandum or record that:
   1. Concerns an issue the witness had knowledge about, but can no longer remember enough to testify fully and accurately.
and 2. Was made or recorded when the issue was fresh in the mind of the witness.
and 3. Correctly represents the witness's knowledge.
  b. If admitted, the memorandum or record may be read into evidence but may not be submitted as an exhibit (unless offered by an adverse party).

**(6) Records of regularly conducted activity.**
  a. <u>Records are not hearsay if</u>:
   1. <u>They are one of the following items</u>:
      A. Memoranda.
or B. Reports.
or C. Records.
or D. Data compilations (in any form).
and 2. <u>They record</u>:
      A. Acts.
or B. Events.
or C. Conditions.
or D. Opinions.
or E. Diagnoses.
and 3. <u>They are recorded</u>:
      A. By a person with knowledge.
or B. From information communicated by a person with knowledge.
and 4. The item was kept in the course of a regularly conducted business activity.

and 5. <u>When recorded</u>: Made at or near the time of the act or event.

and 6. It is regular practice of that business activity to make such records, etc.

and 7. All of the above (1-6) must be shown by the <u>custodian</u> of the records or some <u>other qualified witness</u>, *unless* there is a lack of trustworthiness (as shown by the source of information or the method or circumstances of preparation), in which case the evidence would be <u>inadmissible</u>.

This can also be shown by a <u>Rule 902(11) certification</u>, a <u>Rule 902(12) certification</u>, or by <u>a statute permitting certification</u> (e.g., 18 U.S.C. §3505: "Foreign Records in Criminal Cases").*

b. **"Business"** means a profit/nonprofit business, institution, association, profession, occupation, or calling of any kind.

**(7) Absence of entry in records kept in accordance with the provisions of paragraph (6).**

a. <u>This includes</u>: Evidence that shows that a matter never occurred/existed because:

1. It is normally included in a paragraph (6) record or report.

and 2. It is not included.

b. <u>Exception</u>: If the sources of information or other circumstances indicate lack of trustworthiness, then this type of evidence is <u>inadmissible</u>.

**(8) Public records and reports.**

a. <u>Public records and reports are not hearsay if</u>:

1. They are one of the following items:

A. Records.

or B. Reports.

or C. Statements.

or D. Data compilations (in any form).

and 2. <u>They are recorded by</u>:

A. Public offices.

or B. Public agencies.

and 3. <u>They record the following material</u>:

(A) The office's/agency's <u>activities.</u>

or (B) Matters that the office or agency observed and had to report on by duty of law *unless* they are matters observed by police officers/other law enforcement personnel in criminal cases.

or (C) <u>Factual findings</u> are admissible in civil cases and against the government in criminal cases if

---

*This point was amended December 1, 2000, to add ways of satisfying the 803(6) foundation requirements without the expense and inconvenience of time-consuming foundation witnesses.

produced by an investigation that was conducted with legal authority.

b. <u>Exception</u>: If the sources of information or other circumstances are not trustworthy.

**(9) Records of vital statistics.**

a. <u>Items included</u>: Records/data compilations (in any form) of:

1. Births.
2. Fetal deaths.
3. Deaths.
4. Marriages.

b. <u>Requirements</u>:

1. The report was made <u>to a public office</u>.
and 2. The report was made <u>pursuant to requirements of law</u>.

**(10) Absence of public record or entry.**

a. <u>This includes</u>: Evidence proving the absence of:

1. Records.
2. Reports.
3. Statements.
4. Data compilation (in any form).
5. Nonexistence of a matter of which public records are regularly made and preserved.

b. <u>Requirement</u>: Evidence of the absence may either be:

1. A Rule 902 certification.
or 2. Testimony that after a *diligent search* no record, etc., was found.

**(11) Records of religious organizations.**

The hearsay rule does not apply to statements of the following in a <u>regularly kept record</u> of a religious organization:

a. Births.
b. Marriages.
c. Divorces.
d. Deaths.
e. Legitimacy.
f. Ancestry.
g. Relationship by blood or marriage.
h. Other similar facts of personal/family history.

**(12) Marriage, baptismal, and similar certificates.**

a. This includes statements of fact contained in a certificate that the maker:

1. Performed a marriage.
or 2. Performed some other ceremony.
or 3. Administered a sacrament.

b. These statements must have been made by:

1. A clergyman.

or 2. A public official.

or 3. Another person authorized by a religious organization or by law to perform the act.

c. **Time of statement**. Statement must have been made *either*:

1. At the time of the act.

or 2. At a reasonable time after the act.

(13) **Family records.**

a. This includes statements concerning personal or family history.

b. These are statements that are contained in:

1. Family Bibles.
2. Genealogies.
3. Charts.
4. Engravings on rings.
5. Inscriptions on family portraits.
6. Engravings on urns, crypts or tombstones.
7. Other similar items.

(14) **Records of documents affecting an interest in property.**

a. These are records proving:

1. The **content** of an original document intended to establish or affect a property interest.

and 2. The **execution** and **delivery** of the original document by each person who the document says executed it.

b. Requirements:

1. The record used as evidence must be a record of a public office.

and 2. An applicable statute must authorize the recording of that kind of document in that office.

(15) **Statements in documents affecting an interest in property.**

a. This includes statements in paragraph (14) records that are relevant to the purpose of the document.

b. Exception: When dealings with the property (since the document was made) have been inconsistent with the truth of the statement or the document's substance and intent.

(16) **Statements in ancient documents.**

These are statements in documents that are:

a. Over 20 years old.

and b. Authentic (See Rule 901(b)(8)).

(17) **Market reports, commercial publications.**

a. Items included:

1. Market quotations.
2. Tabulations.
3. Lists.
4. Directories.

5. Other published compilations.
   b. <u>Requirement</u>: Items must be generally used and relied upon by:
      1. The public.
   or 2. Persons in particular occupations.

(18) **Learned treatises.**
   a. <u>Items included</u>: Statements in:
      1. Published treatises.
   or 2. Periodicals.
   or 3. Pamphlets.
   b. <u>Subject matter of items must be</u>:
      1. History.
   or 2. Medicine.
   or 3. Another science or art.
   c. <u>Requirements</u>:
      1. The statement must be:
         a. <u>Called to the attention</u> of an expert witness on cross-examination.
      or b. <u>Relied upon</u> by the expert witness in direct examination.
      2. The item must be a reliable authority as shown by:
         a. The testimony of the witness.
      or b. Admission of the witness.
      or c. Other expert testimony.
      or d. Judicial notice.
   d. If admitted, these statements <u>may be read</u> into evidence but <u>may not be submitted</u> as an exhibit.

(19) **Reputation concerning personal or family history.**
   a. The <u>hearsay rule does not apply to **reputation** concerning a person's</u>:
      1. Birth.
      2. Adoption.
      3. Marriage.
      4. Divorce.
      5. Death.
      6. Legitimacy.
      7. Relationship by blood, adoption, or marriage.
      8. Ancestry.
      9. Similar personal or family history.
   b. <u>This includes reputation among</u>:
      1. Family members by blood, adoption, or marriage.
   or 2. Associates.
   or 3. The community.

**(20) Reputation concerning boundaries or general history.**

The hearsay rule does not apply to reputation in a community (arising before the controversy) as to:

    1. Boundaries of lands in the community.

    2. Customs affecting lands in the community.

    3. Events of general history that are important to the community (or state or nation where the community is located).

**(21) Reputation as to character.**

The hearsay rule does not apply to reputation of a person's character among:

    1. Associates.

or  2. The community.

**(22) Judgment of previous conviction.**

  a. The hearsay rule does not apply to <u>evidence of judgments</u> used to prove any fact if:

    1. Judgment is <u>final</u>.

  and 2. Judgment was entered *either*:

      a. After a trial.

    or  b. After a guilty plea (not a *nolo contendere* plea — see Rule 410).

  and 3. The crime adjudged has a penalty of *either*:

      a. Death.

    or  b. More than one year in prison.

  and 4. <u>Requirement</u>: The fact to be proved must be one that was *essential to sustain the judgment*.

  b. This <u>does not include</u> judgments against persons other than the accused that are:

    1. Offered by the government as evidence.

  and 2. Offered in a criminal prosecution.

  and 3. Offered for purposes other than impeachment.

  c. The pendency of an appeal may be shown but has no effect on admissibility.

**(23) Judgment as to personal, family, or general history, or boundaries.**

  a. The hearsay rule does not apply to judgments used to prove the following matters:

    1. Personal, family, or general history.

    2. Boundaries.

  b. <u>Requirements</u>:

    1. The matter must have been essential to the judgment.

  and 2. The matter would be provable by evidence of reputation (see Rules 19, 20, 21).

**Summary of Advisory Committee's Notes on Rule 803**

Under certain circumstances a hearsay statement may be trustworthy enough to justify not having the declarant appear in person at the trial (even though he may be available). This rule is a synthesis of the exceptions to the hearsay rule, *where the presence of the declarant is immaterial.* The following exceptions apply:

- Exception (1): When an <u>event and a statement are substantially contemporaneous</u>, there is no likelihood of misrepresentation. Moreover, if the witness is the declarant, he may be examined on the statement. If the witness is not the declarant, he may be examined as to the circumstances as an aid in evaluating the statement. Permissible subject matter of the statement is limited to description or explanation of the event or condition.
- Exception (2): When circumstances may produce <u>excitement that temporarily stops a person from reflecting</u>, who instead makes utterances free of conscious fabrication. In this exception, the statement need only "relate" to the startling event or circumstance.
- Exception (3): is an application of Exception (1). The exclusion of "*statements of memory or belief to prove the fact remembered or believed*" is necessary to avoid the harm that would result from allowing state of mind, provable by a hearsay statement, to infer the happening of the event that produced the state of mind.
- Exception (4): <u>Statements of present condition</u> are allowed if made to a physician for *purposes of diagnosis and treatment*. This is in view of the patient's strong motivation to tell the truth. The same goes for statements of past conditions and medical history, as well as causation, made for purposes of diagnosis or treatment. Statements as to fault do not fall under this language (e.g., a patient's statement that he was struck by an automobile would qualify but not his statement that the car was driven through a red light). The statement does not have to be made to a physician. Statements to hospital attendants, ambulance drivers, or even members of the family might be included.
- Exception (5): A <u>record made while events were still fresh in mind</u> and that accurately reflects those events is inherently reliable. The rule here does not spell out the method of establishing the initial knowledge of the witness or that the record was made at the time of the event. They are dealt with according to the particular circumstances of the case.
- Exception (6): <u>Business records</u> are usually very reliable because of systematic checking, regularity, and continuity, which produce habits of precision. Most businesses indeed rely on the records, and make accurate record keeping a duty as part of a continuing job or occupation.
  - The phrase "*the course of a regularly conducted activity*," as well as the broad definition of "business" shows the emphasis on routineness and repetitiveness.
  - All participants, including an observer or participant giving the information are valid sources for the information, as long as they were acting routinely and under a duty of accuracy, with employer reliance on the result, or in short "*in the regular course of business.*"
  - If, however, the supplier of the information does not act in the regular course, there is no assurance of accuracy as to the information (e.g., police report incorporating information obtained from a bystander: the officer qualifies as acting in the regular course but the informant does not).

- The rule describes "record" broadly as a "memorandum, report, record, or data compilation, in any form." The expression "data compilation" is any means of storing information other than the conventional words and figures in written or documentary form. It includes electronic computer storage.
- Exception (7): If a record does not mention a matter that would ordinarily be mentioned, that is evidence of its nonexistence.
- Exception (8): <u>Public records</u> are also excepted. It can be assumed that a public official will perform her duty properly, and it is unlikely that she will remember details independently of the record.
- Exception (9): <u>Records of vital statistics</u> are admissible in evidence.
- Exception (10): The principle of Exception (7) is extended here to public records of the kind mentioned in Exceptions [paragraphs] (8) and (9).
- Exception (11): <u>Records of activities of religious organizations</u> are admissible at least to the extent of the business records exception to the hearsay rule. However, both the business record doctrine and Exception (6) require that the person giving the information be a person in the business or activity (e.g., See <u>Daily v. Grand Lodge</u>, 142 N.E. 478 (1924), holding a church record admissible to prove fact, date, and place of baptism, but not age of child except that he had at least been born at the time). The rule does not require that the informant be in the course of the activity, since it is unlikely that false information would be furnished on occasions of this kind.
- Exception (12): This exception covers the <u>certification procedure to clergymen</u> and the like who perform marriages and other ceremonies or administer sacraments (certificates of baptism or confirmation, as well as marriage, are included).
- Exception (13): <u>Records of family history kept in family Bibles</u> have always been received in evidence (e.g., recognizing family Bible entries as proof of age in the absence of public or church records, using inscriptions on tombstones, publicly displayed pedigrees, and engravings on rings).
- Exception (14): The <u>recording of title documents</u> is admissible. The rule requires that a specified procedure, either acknowledgment or a form of probate, be executed and delivered.
- Exception (15): Under this rule, <u>certain recitals of fact in dispositive documents</u> are exempted from the hearsay rule (e.g., a deed purporting to have been executed by an attorney in fact may recite the existence of the power of attorney, or a deed may recite that the grantors are all the heirs of the last record owner). They are considered trustworthy because of the circumstances under which the documents are executed and the requirement that the recital be relevant to the purpose of the document.
- Exception (16): <u>Recitals in ancient deeds</u> are a "*limited*" hearsay exception. The danger of mistake is minimized by authentication requirements, and age affords assurance that the writing antedates the present controversy.
- Exception (17): Some other kinds of <u>publications</u> (e.g., newspaper market reports, telephone directories, and city directories) are considered trustworthy because of the general reliance by the public or by a particular segment of it, and the motivation of the person compiling it to be accurate.
- Exception (18): Since it is likely that a treatise will be misunderstood and misapplied without expert assistance and supervision, the rule limits the use of treatises as *substantive evidence* to situations in which an expert is on the stand and can

explain and assist in applying the treatise. The rule also limits the use of a treatise to when the publication itself is physically received in evidence.

- Exceptions (19), (20), and (21): Reputation is considered trustworthy when the topic is the kind that the people of the community inquire about and discuss (e.g., reputation as to land boundaries, customs, general history, character, and marriage).
- Exception (19) deals with matters of <u>personal and family history</u>.
- Exception (20) requires that the reputation come before the controversy, unless the subject matter has some historical character.
- Exception (21) accepts reputation evidence as a means of proving human character.
- Exception (22): When the status of a former judgment is under consideration in subsequent litigation, there are three possibilities that must be noted:
  - **(1)** The <u>*former judgment*</u> is conclusive under the doctrine of *res judicata* (either as a bar or as collateral estoppel).
  - or **(2)** It is admissible in evidence for what it is worth.
  - or **(3)** It may be of no effect at all.
- The rule does not deal with the substantive effect of the judgment as a bar or collateral estoppel. When the doctrine of *res judicata* does not apply, however, there is a choice between the second and third alternatives.
- <u>Minor Offenses</u>: Practical considerations require the exclusion of convictions of minor offenses because people often defend themselves at this level with only minimal or no effort (not because the administration of justice in its lower echelons must be inferior).
- Judgments of convictions based upon pleas or *nolo contendere* are not included.
- Exception (23): The process of inquiry, sifting, and scrutiny that we rely upon to render reputation reliable is present in great measure in the process of litigation.

# Rule 804. Hearsay Exceptions; Declarant Unavailable

(a) **Definition of unavailability.**
   i. A declarant is "unavailable as a witness" where the declarant:
      (1) Is exempt because the subject matter of his statement is privileged.
      or (2) Persists in refusing to testify (even after court orders to do so).
      or (3) Testifies to a lack of memory.
      or (4) Is dead or suffers a physical or mental sickness.
      or (5) Is absent <u>and</u> the user of the statement cannot bring the declarant in (or declarant's testimony for 804(b)(2), (3), or (4)) by *reasonable means*.
   ii. <u>Exception</u>: Where the above is a result of the *user's* wrongdoing intended to prevent a declarant from attending.

(b) **Hearsay exceptions**.
   The hearsay rule does not apply to the following (if the declarant is unavailable as a witness):

(1) **Former testimony.**
    a. When testimony was given *either*:
        1. As a witness at another hearing in the same or a different case.
      or 2. In a deposition taken during the same or another case.
    b. Requirement:
        1. The current adverse party had to have a chance and similar motive then (i.e., when the testimony was formerly given) to develop the testimony by direct, cross, or redirect examination.
        2. In civil cases, it suffices that a predecessor in interest to the adverse party now had a chance and motive.

(2) **Statement under belief of impending death**: This statement must be:
    a. Made by declarant who believed that she was about to die.
  and b. Concerning the cause or circumstances of the expected death.
  and c. In *either*:
        1. A civil action or proceeding.
      or 2. A prosecution for homicide.

(3) **Statement against interest.**
    a. Types of statements this refers to:
        1. A statement so far against the declarant's financial interest.
      or 2. A statement tending to subject the declarant to civil or criminal liability.
      or 3. A statement tending to show that the declarant's claim against another is invalid.
      or 4. A statement offered to exonerate the accused by exposing the declarant to criminal liability, only if supporting circumstances show that the statement is trustworthy.
    b. Required standard: *A reasonable person in the same position* would not have made the statement unless he believed it was true.

(4) **Statement of personal or family history**.
    This includes statements:
    (A) Concerning the declarant's:
        1. Birth.
      or 2. Adoption.
      or 3. Marriage.
      or 4. Divorce.
      or 5. Legitimacy.

or 6. Ancestry.

or 7. Relationship by blood, adoption, or marriage.

or 8. Other similar facts of personal/family history (even if the declarant had no way to obtain personal knowledge of the matter stated).

or (B) Concerning 1-8 above, or death of another person, if the declarant was:

1. Related by blood, adoption, or marriage.

or 2. Intimately associated with the other's family (i.e., she was likely to have accurate information concerning the issue).

(5) **Other exceptions.**

*This subsection was deleted and moved to Rule 807 (with subsection (24) of Rule 803).*

(6) **Forfeiture by wrongdoing.**

A statement offered against a party, where:

a. The party was involved in wrongdoing that was intended to make the declarant unavailable as a witness.

and b. The wrongdoing actually did make the declarant unavailable.

# Rule 805. Hearsay within Hearsay

The hearsay rule does not apply to **"hearsay within hearsay"** if <u>each part</u> of the combined statements satisfies an exception to the hearsay rule (one of the exceptions in Rules 803 or 804).

---

**Summary of Advisory Committee's Notes on Rule 805**

The hearsay rule excludes a hearsay statement that includes a further hearsay statement when both fit the requirements of a hearsay exception (e.g., a hospital record might contain an entry of the patient's age based on information given by his wife; this would be a regular entry except that the person who gave the information was not acting in the routine of the business. However, her statement independently qualifies as a statement made for purposes of diagnosis or treatment, and hence each of the two statements falls under an exception).

---

# Rule 806. Attacking and Supporting Credibility of Declarant

a. <u>This rule applies when</u>:

1. Hearsay statements are admitted into evidence.

2. Statements defined in Rule 801(d)(2)(C), (D), and (E) are admitted into evidence.

b. The credibility of the declarant may be attacked/supported by any evidence that would be admissible had the declarant testified as a witness.

c. The declarant does not have to be given a chance to <u>deny</u> or <u>explain</u> any evidence of her statement or conduct.

d. If a party against whom a hearsay statement has been admitted calls the declarant as a witness, the party may examine the declarant on the statement as if under cross-examination.

---

**Summary of Advisory Committee's Notes on Rule 806**

- This rule provides that whenever a hearsay statement is admitted, the credibility of the declarant of the statement may be attacked. If it is attacked, it may be supported by any evidence that would be admissible for those purposes if the declarant had testified as a witness.
- The main difference between using hearsay and an actual witness is that in the case of the witness an inconsistent statement will almost always be a prior statement, which can be called to the witness's attention. In the case of hearsay, however, the inconsistent statement may be a subsequent one, which makes it practically impossible to call it to the attention of the declarant.
- The rule dispenses with this requirement in all hearsay situations, which is readily administered and best calculated to lead to fair results.

---

## Rule 807. Residual Exception
(Effective December 1, 1997)

*This is a relatively new rule that consists of former Rules 803(24) and 804(b)(5).* Other statements (not covered by 803 or 804) are not excluded by the hearsay rule if the court determines that:

(A) The statement is offered as evidence of a material fact.

and (B) The statement is the <u>best evidence</u> that the user can obtain through *reasonable efforts.*

and (C) Admitting the statement will best serve *the general purpose of these rules* and *the interests of justice.*

and (D) The evidence has an equivalent "guarantee of trustworthiness" as the other exceptions in Rules 803 and 804.

and (E) The user of the evidence notifies the adverse party in advance (to provide a fair opportunity to prepare) of the:
1. **Intention** to use the statement.
2. **Specifics** of the statement, including the declarant's name and address.

# ARTICLE IX
# AUTHENTICATION AND IDENTIFICATION

## Rule 901. Requirement of Authentication or Identification

(a) **General provision.**

1. **Authentication** or **identification** is required as a condition precedent to admissibility.
2. This requirement is satisfied by "evidence sufficient to support a finding that the matter in question is what its proponent claims."

(b) **Illustrations:** The following are merely examples (not limitations) of **authentication** or **identification**.

 (1) <u>**Testimony of witness with knowledge**</u>: Testimony that a matter is what it is claimed to be is sufficient for authentication.

 (2) <u>**Nonexpert opinion on handwriting**</u>: The opinion may be used to authenticate handwriting so long as it is based upon familiarity not obtained for purposes of the litigation.

 (3) <u>**Comparison by trier or expert witness**</u>: For authentication/identification, it is sufficient to compare with specimens that have been authenticated.

 (4) <u>**Distinctive characteristics and the like**</u>: The following characteristics may be used so long as they are taken in conjunction with the circumstances:

  a. Appearance.
  b. Contents.
  c. Substance.
  d. Internal patterns.
  e. Other distinctive characteristics.

 (5) <u>**Voice identification can be used if**</u>:

  a. <u>Voices that can be identified can be heard *either*</u>:

   1. Firsthand.
   or 2. Through mechanical or electronic transmission.
   or 3. Through mechanical or electronic recording.

  and b. The opinion of the voice identification is based on hearing the voice under circumstances connecting it with the alleged speaker.

 (6) <u>**Telephone conversations**</u> can be authenticated if:

  i. Evidence is provided that a call was made to the number assigned at that time to a particular person/business.

  and ii. *Either*:

      (A) <u>Person</u>: Circumstances (including self-identification) show that the person who answered was the one called.

or  (B) <u>Business</u>:
      1. The call was made to a place of business.
  and 2. The conversation related to business that is usually done over the phone.

(7) **Public records or reports** can be authenticated with evidence that a writing is from the public office where such items are recorded or kept.

(8) **Ancient documents or data compilation** can be authenticated with evidence that they are:
    (A) In a condition raising no suspicion as to their authenticity.
  and (B) In a place where authentic documents are likely to be.
  and (C) Over 20 years old.

(9) **Process or system** may be identified with evidence describing the process and showing that it produces an accurate result.

(10) **Methods provided by statute or rule**. Authentication may also be done as provided for by:
    a. Act of Congress.
  or b. Other rules prescribed by the U.S. Supreme Court pursuant to statutory authority.

---

**Summary of Advisory Committee's Notes on Rule 901**

- Today there are procedures such as <u>requests to admit</u> and <u>pretrial conferences</u> that eliminate much of the need for authentication or identification. Also, accepting items of the kind in Rule 902 as at least prima facie genuine, has also done this. However, the need for suitable methods of proof still remains, for the following reasons:
  - **(a)** Criminal cases have their own obstacles to the use of preliminary procedures.
  - and **(b)** Unforeseen contingencies may arise.
  - and **(c)** Cases of genuine controversy still occur.
- The examples in subdivision (b) are not intended as an exclusive list of allowable methods but are meant to guide and suggest, leaving room for growth and development in this area of the law.
- The examples relate for the most part to documents, with some attention given to voice communications and computer printouts. Note that compliance with requirements of authentication or identification does not guarantee that an item will be admitted into evidence, as other bars — hearsay for example — may remain.
  - Example (1) ranges from testimony of a witness who was present at the signing of a document to testimony establishing narcotics as taken from an accused and accounting for custody through the period until trial, including laboratory analysis.
  - Example (2) recognizes that one may be able to later recognize the handwriting of another person by seeing him write, by exchanging correspondence, or by other means. Testimony based upon familiarity acquired for purposes of the litigation is reserved to the expert under Example (3).

- Example (3) sets no higher standard for handwriting specimens and treats all comparison situations alike, to be governed by Rule 104(b). Visual comparison sufficiently satisfies the preliminary authentication requirements for admission in evidence.
- Example (4) indicates that the characteristics of the offered item itself may afford authentication techniques (e.g., a document or telephone conversation may be shown to have emanated from a particular person if it discloses knowledge of facts known peculiarly to him; a letter may be authenticated by content and circumstances indicating it was in reply to a duly authenticated one; language patterns may indicate authenticity or its opposite).
- Example (5) maintains that since oral voice identification is not a subject of expert testimony, one may become familiar with a voice either before or after the particular speaking that is the subject of the identification (this is similar to visual identification of a person, and unlike identification of handwriting).
- Example (6) indicates that usual conduct respecting telephone calls furnishes adequate assurances of regularity. The matter, however, is open to exploration before the trier of fact. Public records are regularly authenticated by proof of custody, without more.
- Example (7) extends the principle to include data stored in computers and similar methods, which are increasingly being used in the public records area.
- Example (8) extends the ancient document rule to include data stored electronically or by other similar means. The importance of custody or place where found increases as the importance of appearance decreases. The expansion of this example is necessary in view of the widespread use of methods of storing data in forms other than conventional written records.
- Example (9) is designed for situations in which the accuracy of a result is dependent upon a process or system that produces it (e.g., X-rays; computers). Example (9) does not, of course, foreclose taking judicial notice of the accuracy of the process or system.
- Example (10) says that methods of authentication provided by act of Congress and by the Rules of Civil and Criminal Procedure or by Bankruptcy Rules are not intended to be superseded (e.g., provisions for authentication of official records in Civil Procedure Rule 44 and Criminal Procedure Rule 27; provisions for authentication of records of proceedings by court reporters in 28 U.S.C. §753(b) and Civil Procedure Rule 80(c); provisions for authentication of depositions in Civil Procedure Rule 30(f)).

## Rule 902. Self-Authentication

The following do not need outside evidence for authentication:

(1) **Domestic public documents under seal.** If a document has:
  a. A seal of:
    1. The United States.
    or 2. Any state, district, commonwealth, or territory.
    or 3. Any insular possession of a state, district, commonwealth, or territory.
    or 4. The Panama Canal Zone.
    or 5. The Trust Territory of the Pacific Islands.

or 6. Any political subdivision, department, officer, or agency of the above-listed

and b. A signature purporting to be an attestation or execution.

(2) **Domestic public documents not under seal.** If a document has <u>no seal</u>, but:

    1. It purports to have the signature of an officer or employee of an entity listed in (1).

    and 2. A public officer who (has a seal and official duties in the district of the officer) certifies under seal that:

        a. The signer has the official capacity.

        and b. The signature is genuine.

(3) **Foreign public documents** purporting to be executed and attested by an official may be self-authenticated if they are accompanied by:

    i. A certification as to the genuineness of the signature and official position of:

        (A) The person executing or attesting to the document.

        or (B) Any foreign official whose certificate of genuineness of signature and official position somehow relates to the execution or attestation.

    ii. The certification may be made by:

        a. A secretary of an embassy or legation.

        or b. Consul general.

        or c. Consul.

        or d. Vice consul.

        or e. Consular agent of the United States.

        or f. A U.S.-assigned diplomatic or consular official of the foreign country.

    iii. If all parties have been given reasonable opportunity to check the authenticity, the court may, _for good cause shown_:

        1. Order that they are _presumed authentic_ without certification.

        or 2. Permit them to be evidenced by an attested summary (even without certification).

(4) **Certified copies of public records.**

    a. This includes:

        1. Copies of official records or reports (or an entry in a record or report).

        2. Copies of documents authorized by law to be recorded or filed (and actually recorded or filed), including data compilations.

    b. These must be certified as correct by an authorized person:

        1. By certificate complying with 902(1), (2), and (3).

        or 2. By complying with an act of Congress.

        or 3. By complying with other rules prescribed by the U.S. Supreme Court pursuant to statutory authority.

(5) **Official publications** purporting to be issued by public authority, including:
- a. Books.
- b. Pamphlets.
- c. Other publications.

(6) **Newspapers and periodicals.** Printed materials purporting to be newspapers or periodicals.

(7) **Trade inscriptions and the like,** if:
- a. The trade inscriptions, etc.:
  - 1. Purport to have been fixed in the course of business.
  - and 2. Indicate ownership, control, or origin.
- b. "Trade inscriptions" includes:
  - 1. Inscriptions.
  - and 2. Signs.
  - and 3. Tags.
  - and 4. Labels.

(8) **Acknowledged documents.** Documents accompanied by an acknowledgment executed:
- 1. In a manner provided by law.
- 2. By a notary public or other authorized officer.

(9) **Commercial paper and related documents.** This includes:
- 1. Commercial paper.
- and 2. Signatures on commercial paper.
- and 3. Documents relating to commercial paper (to the extent provided by general commercial law).

(10) **Presumptions under Acts of Congress.**
"Any signature, document, or other matter declared by Act of Congress to be presumptively or prima facie genuine or authentic."

(11) **Certified domestic records of regularly conducted activity.**
- a. If a domestic record of regularly conducted activity would be admissible under 803(6) (see Amendment), the original or duplicate of that record would be admissible, so long as it is accompanied by a <u>written declaration</u> (by the custodian or some other qualified witness) certifying the following:
  - (A) The record was made at or near the time of the occurrence of the matters set forth by (or from information transmitted by) a person with knowledge of those matters.
  - and (B) The record was made in the course of *regularly conducted activity*.
  - and (C) The record was made by the regularly conducted activity *as a regular practice*.

      b. The written declaration is to be made in such a way that complies with any act of Congress or rule prescribed by the Supreme Court (pursuant to statutory authority) (e.g., 28 U.S.C. § 1746).

      c. A party offering a record into evidence under Rule 902(11) must:

         1. Provide written notice to all adverse parties.

    and 2. Make the record and the declaration available for inspection in advance of the offer into evidence (sufficient to provide an adverse party a fair opportunity to challenge the foundation set forth in the declaration).

**(12) Certified foreign records of regularly conducted activity.**

      a. If a foreign record of regularly conducted activity would be admissible under 803(6) (see Amendment), the original or duplicate of that record would be admissible, so long as it is accompanied by a <u>written declaration</u> (by the custodian or some other qualified witness) certifying the following:

         (A) The record was made at or near the time of the occurrence of the matters set forth by (or from information transmitted by) a person with knowledge of those matters.

    and (B) The record was made in the course of *regularly conducted activity.*

    and (C) The record was made by the regularly conducted activity *as a regular practice.*

      b. This subsection applies only in <u>civil cases</u>.

      c. The declaration must be signed in such a way that if the declaration is false, the maker would be subject to criminal penalty under the laws of the country where the declaration was made.

      d. A party offering a record into evidence under Rule 902(11) must:

         1. Provide written notice to all adverse parties.

    and 2. Make the record and the declaration available for inspection in advance of the offer into evidence (sufficient to provide an adverse party a fair opportunity to challenge the foundation set forth in the declaration).

---

**Summary of Advisory Committee's Notes on Rule 902**

- This rule collects the situations in which authenticity is taken as *sufficiently established* for purposes of admissibility without extrinsic evidence to that effect. The reasons for this are reasons of policy, and also because practical considerations greatly reduce the possibility of unauthenticity.
- The opposite party is never prevented from disputing authenticity.
- The acceptance of documents bearing a <u>public seal and signature</u> is most often encountered in practice while in the form of acknowledgments or certificates authenticating copies of public records.

- Paragraph (2) calls for authentication by an officer who has a seal. Notarial acts by members of the armed forces and other special situations are covered in paragraph (10). This is because of the ease of forgery.
- Paragraph (3) provides a method for extending the presumption of authenticity to foreign official documents by a procedure of certification. It is derived from Rule 44(a)(2) of the Rules of Civil Procedure but is not limited to public records.
- Documents provable when presented in original form under paragraphs (1), (2), or (3) may not be provable by certified copy under paragraph (4).
- Paragraph (5) does not admit all official publications; it merely provides a means whereby the authenticity of the publications may be taken as established for purposes of admissibility.
- Paragraph (6) is based on the idea that the likelihood of forgery of newspapers or periodicals is slight. Establishing the authenticity of the publication may, of course, leave still open questions of authority and responsibility for items contained in the publication.
- Paragraph (7) discusses the risk of forgery of commercial and mercantile labels and the like, which is minimal. Trademark infringement involves serious penalties. Great efforts are devoted to inducing the public to buy in reliance on brand names, and substantial protection is given them.
- Paragraph (8) conforms to the rule in virtually every state, where title documents are receivable in evidence without further proof. If this authentication is enough for documents as important as those affecting titles, the same should be true when other kinds of documents are involved.
- Paragraph (10) dispenses with preliminary proof of genuineness where provided in various acts of Congress (e.g., 10 U.S.C. §936, signature, without seal, together with title, are prima facie evidence of authenticity of acts of certain military personnel who are given notarial power; 15 U.S.C. §77f(a), signature on SEC registration presumed genuine; 26 U.S.C. §6064, signature to tax return prima facie genuine).
- Paragraphs (11) and (12) were added in a December 1, 2000, amendment.

# Rule 903. Subscribing Witness' Testimony Unnecessary

A subscribing witness's <u>testimony is not necessary</u> to authenticate a writing, *unless* required by the jurisdictional laws (whose laws govern the writing's validity).

**Summary of Advisory Committee's Notes on Rule 903**
The requirement that attesting witnesses be produced or accounted for has generally been abolished except with respect to documents that must be attested to be valid (e.g., wills in some states).

# ARTICLE X
# CONTENTS OF WRITINGS, RECORDINGS, AND PHOTOGRAPHS

## Rule 1001. Definitions

(1) **"Writings and recordings."**
- a. <u>Writings and recordings consist of</u>:
  - 1. Letters.
  - or 2. Words.
  - or 3. Numbers.
  - or 4. Their equivalent.
- b. <u>Form</u>:
  - 1. Handwriting.
  - 2. Typewriting.
  - 3. Printing.
  - 4. Photostatting.
  - 5. Photographing.
  - 6. Magnetic impulse.
  - 7. Mechanical or electronic recording.
  - 8. Other form of data compilation.

(2) **"Photographs"** include:
- a. Still photographs.
- b. X-ray films.
- c. Video tapes.
- d. Motion pictures.

(3) **"Original."**
- a. <u>Writings and recordings</u>:
  - 1. A writing or recording itself.
  - or 2. Any counterpart intended to have the same effect by a person executing or issuing it.
- b. <u>Photographs</u>:
  - 1. The negative.
  - or 2. A print from the negative.
- c. <u>Computer-stored data</u>:
  - 1. Any accurate printout.
  - or 2. Any other accurate output readable by sight.

(4) **"Duplicate"** is a counterpart produced:
- a. By the same impression as the original.
- or b. From the same matrix as the original.
- or c. By means of photography (including enlargements and miniatures).

or  d.  By mechanical or electronic rerecording.

or  e.  By chemical reproduction.

or  f.  By other equivalent techniques that are accurate.

**Summary of Advisory Committee's Notes on Rule 1001**

- Important areas of usefulness of the *"best evidence rule"* are when discovery of documents outside the jurisdiction may require substantial outlay of time and money; the unanticipated document may not practically be discoverable; criminal cases have built-in limitations on discovery.
- Paragraph (1) expands the rule to include computers, photographic systems, and other modern developments.
- Paragraph (3) shows some cases where a particularized definition for an "original" is required (e.g., a carbon copy of a contract executed in duplicate and a sales ticket carbon copy given to a customer become originals; any print from a negative of a photograph is regarded as an original; any computer printout is an original).
- The definition in Paragraph (4) describes "copies" produced by methods that have an accuracy that virtually eliminates the possibility of error. These copies are considered originals in large measure by Rule 1003. Copies subsequently produced manually, whether handwritten or typed, are not within the definition.
- Finally, the rule points out that what is an original for some purposes may be a duplicate for others (e.g., a bank's microfilm record of checks cleared is the original as a record; however, a print offered as a copy of a check whose contents are in controversy is a duplicate).

## Rule 1002. Requirement of Original

The **original** of any writing, recording, or photograph is required to prove its **content**, *unless* provided for by:

1. Act of Congress.

or  2. The FRE.

**Summary of Advisory Committee's Notes on Rule 1002**

- This rule expands the rule requiring production of the original document to prove its contents, to include <u>writings</u>, <u>recordings</u>, and <u>photographs</u>, as defined in Rule 1001(1) and (2).
- Application of this rule depends on whether contents are sought to be proved. An event may be proved by nondocumentary evidence, even though a written record of it was made. If, however, the event is sought to be proved by the written record, this rule applies (e.g., payment may be proved without producing the written receipt that was given; earnings may be proved without producing books of account in which they are entered; testimony that books or records have been examined and found not to contain any reference to a designated matter may prove its nonoccurrence).
- This rule will seldom apply to <u>ordinary photographs</u>. The usual course is for a witness on the stand to identify the photograph or motion picture as a correct representation of events that he saw or of a scene with which he is familiar. In fact he adopts the picture as his testimony, or, in other words, uses the picture to

illustrate his testimony. Since no effort is made to prove the contents of the picture, the rule does not apply. On occasion, however, situations arise in which contents are sought to be proved (e.g., copyright infringement, defamation, and invasion of privacy by photograph or motion picture). There are also some situations in which the picture is offered as having independent probative value (e.g., security camera photograph of bank robber; X-rays), which call for production of the original.

## Rule 1003. Admissibility of Duplicates

A **duplicate** is admissible to the same extent as the **original** *unless*:

(1) There is a *genuine question* as to the authenticity of the original.

or (2) Under the circumstances it would be unfair to allow the copy instead of the original.

---

**Summary of Advisory Committee's Notes on Rule 1003**
- If no genuine issue exists as to authenticity and no other reason exists for requiring the original, a duplicate is admissible under the rule.
- This is because the only concern is with getting the words or other contents before the court accurately. By definition in Rule 1001(4), a "duplicate" possesses this character.
- Reasons for requiring the original may be present when only a part of the original is reproduced and the rest:
    **(a)** Is needed for cross-examination.
    or **(b)** May disclose matters qualifying the part offered.
    or **(c)** May disclose matters otherwise useful to the opposing party.

---

## Rule 1004. Admissibility of Other Evidence of Contents

Other evidence of the content of a writing, recording, or photograph is admissible in place of an original if:

(1) **The originals were lost or destroyed.** All originals are either lost or have been destroyed, *unless* the proponent lost/destroyed them in bad faith.

(2) **The original is not obtainable.** No original can be obtained by any judicial procedure.

(3) **The original is in possession of an opponent.** An opposing party who has possession of the original does not produce it at a hearing, even after receiving notice that its contents would be a subject of proof at a hearing.

(4) **Collateral matters.** The writing, recording, or photograph is not closely related to a controlling issue.

**Summary of Advisory Committee's Notes on Rule 1004**

- This rule specifies when production of the original as proof of contents is excused.
- Basically, if failure to produce the original is satisfactorily explained, secondary evidence is admissible.
- There are no "degrees" of secondary evidence, since the formulation of a hierarchy of preferences would be too complex.
  - Loss or destruction of the original, unless due to bad faith of the proponent, is a satisfactory explanation of nonproduction.
  - Loss or destruction of an original by another person at the instigation of the proponent is considered the same as loss or destruction in bad faith by the proponent himself (see Paragraph (1)).
- When the original is in the possession of a third person, and one cannot get it from her by some judicial procedure, that is sufficient explanation of nonproduction.
- Judicial procedure includes subpoena *duces tecum* as an incident to the taking of a deposition in another jurisdiction. (Paragraph (2)).
- If a party who has an original in his control is put on notice that proof of contents will be made, he does not need further protection by the rule. The notice procedure here provided is not to be confused with orders to produce or other discovery procedures, since the purpose of this rule is to give the opposing party an opportunity to produce the original. It is not meant to compel him to do so (Paragraph (3)). Situations arise in which no good purpose is served by production of the original. These are difficult to determine exactly. Examples are the newspaper in an action for the price of publishing defendant's advertisement, and the streetcar transfer of a plaintiff claiming status as a passenger (Paragraph (4)).

## Rule 1005. Public Records

a. This includes:
  1. Copies of official records.
  2. Copies of documents authorized by law to be recorded or filed (and actually recorded or filed), including data compilations.

b. The contents of (otherwise admissible) public records may be proved by copy that is certified to be correct:
  1. In accordance with Rule 902.
  or 2. By testimony of a witness who has compared the copy with the original.

c. If such a copy cannot be obtained by *reasonable diligence,* then other evidence of the contents may be given.

**Summary of Advisory Committee's Notes on Rule 1005**

Removing public records from their usual place of keeping would seriously inconvenience the public and the custodian. However, not requiring an original to be produced would open the door to the introduction of every kind of secondary evidence of contents of public records. The rule therefore recognizes degrees of secondary evidence in this situation, and gives preference for certified or compared copies.

# Rule 1006. Summaries

a. **Summaries, charts,** or **calculations** may be used to present the contents of voluminous writings, records, or photographs.

b. The originals (or duplicates) must be made available for examination and/or copying by other parties at a reasonable time and place.

c. The court can order that they be produced in court.

> **Summary of Advisory Committee's Notes on Rule 1006**
> The only practicable way of making the contents of voluminous books, records, or documents available to judge and jury is the admission of summaries. The rule recognizes this practice, with appropriate safeguards.

# Rule 1007. Testimony or Written Admission of Party

The following can always be used to prove the contents of writings, recordings, or photographs without producing an original:

1. **Testimony** of the adverse party.

2. **Deposition** of the adverse party.

3. The adverse party's **written admission.**

> **Summary of Advisory Committee's Notes on Rule 1007**
> The rule gives preference to the original in proving contents, as the risk of inaccuracy is substantial. The use of admissions is limited to those made in the course of giving testimony or in writing. This does not exclude evidence of an oral admission when nonproduction of the original has been accounted for and secondary evidence generally has become admissible. Rule 1004.

# Rule 1008. Functions of Court and Jury

i. When admissibility of <u>other evidence</u> of contents of writings, recordings, or photographs depends on the fulfillment of a condition, **the court determines** (in accordance with Rule 104) whether or not the condition has been fulfilled.

ii. **The trier of fact determines** the following issues (as it does with any other facts):
    (a) Whether the asserted writing ever existed.
    (b) Whether a writing, recording, or photograph produced at trial is the original.
    (c) Whether other evidence of contents correctly reflects the contents.

**Summary of Advisory Committee's Notes on Rule 1008**
The judge decides most preliminary questions of fact that deal with the rule preferring the original as evidence of contents. This follows the general principles of Rule 104. However, questions that go beyond the mere administration of the rule and into the merits of the controversy (e.g., plaintiff offers secondary evidence of the contents of an alleged contract, after first introducing evidence of loss of the original, and defendant counters with evidence that no such contract was ever executed) are left to the jury's determination, subject to the control exercised generally by the judge over jury determinations (see Rule 104(b)).

# ARTICLE XI
# MISCELLANEOUS RULES

## Rule 1101. Applicability of Rules

(a) **Courts and judges.**
1. These rules apply to:
   a. The U.S. district courts.
   b. The District Court of Guam.
   c. The District Court of the Virgin Islands.
   d. The District Court for the Northern Mariana Islands.
   e. The U.S. courts of appeals.
   f. The U.S. Claims Court
   g. U.S. bankruptcy judges.
   h. U.S. magistrate judges.
2. "Judge" and "court" when used in these rules include U.S. bankruptcy judges and U.S. magistrate judges.

(b) **Proceedings generally.**
These rules apply generally to:
1. Civil actions and proceedings (including admiralty and maritime cases).
2. Criminal cases and proceedings.
3. Contempt proceedings (except those in which the court may act summarily).
4. Cases under Title 11 of the U.S. Code.

(c) **Rule of privilege.**
The privilege rules apply at all stages of all actions, cases, and proceedings.

(d) **Rules inapplicable.**
These rules (other than with respect to privileges) do not apply in the following cases:
(1) **Preliminary questions of fact.** Questions of fact preliminary to admissibility of evidence when the issue is to be determined by the court under Rule 104.
(2) **Grand jury proceedings.**
(3) **Miscellaneous Proceedings.**
   a. Proceedings for extradition or rendition.
   b. Preliminary examinations in criminal cases.
   c. Sentencing.
   d. Granting or revoking probation.
   e. Issuance of warrants for arrest.
   f. Issuance of criminal summonses.
   g. Issuance of search warrants.
   h. Proceedings with respect to release (on bail or otherwise).

(e) **Rules applicable in part.**

These rules apply only to the extent that a <u>statute</u> or <u>Supreme Court rule</u> does not provide for matters of evidence in the following proceedings:

1. The trial of misdemeanors and other petty offenses before U.S. magistrate judges.
2. Review of agency actions when the facts are subject to trial *de novo* under 5 U.S.C. §706(2)(F).
3. Review of orders of the secretary of agriculture under section 2 of the act entitled "An Act to authorize association of producers of agricultural products" approved February 18, 1922 (7 U.S.C. §292), and under sections 6 and 7(c) of the Perishable Agricultural Commodities Act, 1930 (7 U.S.C. §§499f, 499g(c)).
4. Naturalization and revocation of naturalization under sections 310-318 of the Immigration and Nationality Act (8 U.S.C. §§1421-1429).
5. Prize proceedings in admiralty under 10 U.S.C. §§7651-7681.
6. Review of orders of the secretary of the interior under section 2 of the act entitled "An Act authorizing associations of producers of aquatic products" approved June 25, 1934 (15 U.S.C. §522).
7. Review of orders of petroleum control boards under section 5 of the act entitled "An Act to regulate interstate and foreign commerce in petroleum and its products by prohibiting the shipment in such commerce of petroleum and its products produced in violation of State law, and for other purposes," approved February 22, 1935 (15 U.S.C. §715d).
8. Actions for fines, penalties, or forfeitures under part V of title IV of the Tariff Act of 1930 (19 U.S.C. §§1581-1624), or under the Anti-Smuggling Act (19 U.S.C. §§1701-1711).
9. Criminal libel for condemnation, exclusion of imports, or other proceedings under the Federal Food, Drug, and Cosmetic Act (21 U.S.C. §§301-392); disputes between seamen under sections 4079, 4080, and 4081 of the Revised Statutes (22 U.S.C. §§256-258).
10. Habeas corpus under 28 U.S.C. §§2241-2254; motions to vacate, set aside or correct sentence under 28 U.S.C. §§2255.
11. Actions for penalties for refusal to transport destitute seamen under section 4578 of the Revised Statutes (46 U.S.C. §679).
12. Actions against the United States under the act entitled "An Act authorizing suits against the United States in admiralty for damage caused by and salvage service rendered to public vessels belonging to the United States, and for other purposes," approved March 3, 1925 (46 U.S.C. §§781-790), as implemented by 10 U.S.C. §7730.

**Summary of Advisory Committee's Notes on Rule 1101**
- Subdivision (a) states the courts and judges to which the Rules of Evidence apply.
- Subdivision (b) is a combination of the language of the Enabling Acts (*supra*) with respect to the kinds of proceedings in which the making of rules is authorized. It is subject to the qualifications expressed in the subdivisions that follow.
- Subdivision (c), singling out the rules of privilege for special treatment, is made necessary by the limited applicability of the remaining rules.
- Subdivision (d) is not intended to be an expression as to when due process or other constitutional provisions may require an evidentiary hearing.

## Rule 1102. Amendments

"Amendments to the Federal Rules of Evidence may be made as provided in section 2072 of Title 28 of the United States Code."

## Rule 1103. Title

"These rules may be known and cited as the Federal Rules of Evidence."

# APPENDIX I

## *E-Z TOOL* for APPROACHING an EVIDENCE PROBLEM

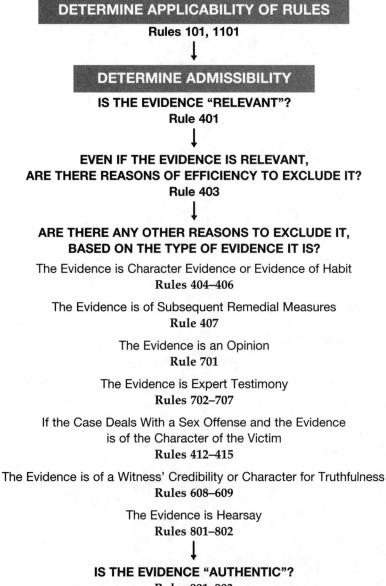

**DETERMINE APPLICABILITY OF RULES**
Rules 101, 1101
↓

**DETERMINE ADMISSIBILITY**
IS THE EVIDENCE "RELEVANT"?
Rule 401
↓

EVEN IF THE EVIDENCE IS RELEVANT,
ARE THERE REASONS OF EFFICIENCY TO EXCLUDE IT?
Rule 403
↓

ARE THERE ANY OTHER REASONS TO EXCLUDE IT,
BASED ON THE TYPE OF EVIDENCE IT IS?

The Evidence is Character Evidence or Evidence of Habit
Rules 404–406

The Evidence is of Subsequent Remedial Measures
Rule 407

The Evidence is an Opinion
Rule 701

The Evidence is Expert Testimony
Rules 702–707

If the Case Deals With a Sex Offense and the Evidence
is of the Character of the Victim
Rules 412–415

The Evidence is of a Witness' Credibility or Character for Truthfulness
Rules 608–609

The Evidence is Hearsay
Rules 801–802
↓

IS THE EVIDENCE "AUTHENTIC"?
Rules 901–903
↓

IF THE EVIDENCE IS A WRITING, RECORDING OR
PHOTOGRAPH, IS THE "BEST EVIDENCE"?
Rules 1001–1004

# APPENDIX II

## *E-Z TOOL* for the FEDERAL RULES of EVIDENCE

| Type of Evidence | Admissible | Inadmissible | Applicable Rule |
|---|---|---|---|
| Admissions by Party-Opponents | • If the statement was made or adopted by the party or by an agent of the party | | Rule 801 |
| Character Evidence | • Describes character of accused and offered by the accused or by the prosecution to rebut<br>• Describes character of victim and offered by the accused or by the prosecution to rebut, or in a homicide case, by the prosecution to prove that victim was not aggressor | • To show that person acted in a certain way<br>• Other crimes or wrongs to show that person acted in a similar way | Rule 404 |
| Evidence of Character of Witness | • Opinion and Reputation evidence will be limited to truthfulness and untruthfulness | | Rule 608(a) |
| Compro-mises or Offers to Compro-mise | To prove:<br>• Bias or prejudice of a witness<br>• The negation of a contention of undue delay<br>• Obstruction of a criminal investigation/ prosecution | To prove:<br>• Liability of a claim<br>• Invalidity of a claim or its amount | Rule 408 |
| Evidence of Conduct of Witness | • May be proved only by what the witness says, so long as instances are probative of truthfulness or untruthfulness<br>• Extrinsic evidence may be used if conduct at issue refers to conviction of a crime | | Rule 608(b) |

*Continued on next page*

| Type of Evidence | Admissible | Inadmissible | Applicable Rule |
|---|---|---|---|
| Evidence of Conviction of Crime | • Convictions of crimes involving dishonesty or falsehood | • If more than 10 years have passed<br>• If conviction was a juvenile adjudication<br>• Witness has been pardoned and had not committed a crime punishable by more than 1 year | Rule 609 |
| Extrinsic Evidence of Prior Statements of Witness | • Witness given a chance to explain/deny the evidence and<br>• Opposing party is given a chance to interrogate the witness on the evidence | | Rule 613 |
| Habit | • To prove conduct on a particular occasion | | Rule 406 |
| Hearsay | | Generally | Rule 802 |
| Hearsay Admissions that are conditioned on the declarant's unavailability | • Former testimony<br>• Statement about cause of injury or illness was made under belief of impending death<br>• Against financial interests or tending to subject declarant to civil/criminal liability<br>• Family history<br>• Other statements that carry a guarantee of trustworthiness | | Rule 804 |
| Hearsay Admissions that do not depend on the availability of the declarant | See Rule 803 | | Rule 803 |

*Continued on next page*

| Type of Evidence | Admissible | Inadmissible | Applicable Rule |
| --- | --- | --- | --- |
| Hearsay within Hearsay | Generally | | Rule 805 |
| Liability Insurance | • To show agency, ownership or control<br>• To show bias or prejudice | • To show negligence or other wrongful act | Rule 411 |
| Payment of Medical Expenses or Offers to Pay | | To prove liability | Rule 409 |
| Pleas, Discussions, Related Statements | • When another statement has been introduced (and it is only fair to consider this with it)<br>• In a proceeding for perjury when statement was made:<br>  ○ Under oath, and<br>  ○ On the record, and<br>  ○ In front of counsel | • Guilty plea that was later withdrawn<br>• *Nolo contendere* plea<br>• Statement regarding the above | Rule 410 |
| Prior Statements by Witnesses | If the statement:<br>• Is inconsistent with the testimony<br>• Is consistent and offered to dispute a charge that the person making the statement lied<br>• Identifies a person | | Rule 801 |
| Religious Beliefs or Opinions | | To prove credibility | Rule 610 |
| Reputation or Opinion Evidence (for proving character) | Only to prove admissible character evidence | | Rule 405 |

*Continued on next page*

| Type of Evidence | Admissible | Inadmissible | Applicable Rule |
|---|---|---|---|
| Sex Offense Cases - Reputation of Alleged Victim | • If constitutionally required to be admitted (412(c)(3) does not apply)<br>• To show past sexual behavior with others for purposes of showing whether or not accused was source of semen or injury (Need 412(c) motion and hearing)<br>• To show past sexual behavior with the accused to prove consent (Need 412(c) motion and hearing)<br>• (New rule) To show past sexual behavior with the accused when offered by the prosecution<br>• (New rule) In civil cases, sexual predisposition if the value outweighs the danger or prejudice, and reputation if the alleged victim placed it in controversy | Evidence of victim's past sexual behavior/sexual predisposition | Rule 412 |
| Similar Crimes of Sexual Assault and Child Molestation (Violent Crime Control Act) | • In a criminal case in which the defendant is accused of that crime<br>• In civil cases in which a claim relies on a party's alleged commission of conduct that constitutes an offense | Evidence of victim's past sexual behavior/sexual predisposition | Rules 413-415 |
| Specific Instances of Conduct (for proving character) | Only if character is essential to a claim or defense | | Rule 405 |
| Subsequent Remedial Measures | To prove:<br>• Ownership<br>• Control<br>• Feasibility of precautionary measures<br>• Impeachment | To prove:<br>• Negligence<br>• Culpable conduct | Rule 407 |

*Continued on next page*

| Type of Evidence | Admissible | Inadmissible | Applicable Rule |
|---|---|---|---|
| Writings, Evidence: Proving Contents of | • Original<br>• Duplicate, unless there is a genuine issue of fact as to authenticity of original<br>• Other evidence if:<br>† Original lost, or<br>† Original not obtainable, or<br>† Original in possession of opponent, or<br>† Writing not closely related to controlling issue | | Rules 1001-1004 |

# APPENDIX III

## *E-Z CHECKLIST* for the
## FEDERAL RULES of EVIDENCE

**Did You Make Sure That . . .**

| | | |
|---|---|---|
| ☑ | The Federal Rules of Evidence apply. | Rules 101, 1101 |
| ☑ | The evidence is "relevant." | Rule 401 |
| ☑ | Even though the evidence is relevant, there are no reasons of efficiency to exclude it. | Rule 403 |
| ☑ | If the evidence is character evidence or evidence of a habit, it is admissible. | Rules 404–406 |
| ☑ | If the evidence is of subsequent remedial measures, it is admissible. | Rule 407 |
| ☑ | If the evidence is an opinion, it is admissible. | Rule 701 |
| ☑ | If the evidence is expert testimony, it is admissible. | Rules 702–705 |
| ☑ | If the case deals with a sex offense and the evidence is of the character of the victim, it is admissible. | Rules 412–415 |
| ☑ | If the evidence is of a witness's "character for truthfulness," it is admissible. | Rules 608–609 |
| ☑ | If the evidence is hearsay, an exception applies. | Rules 801–803 |
| ☑ | The evidence is "authentic." | Rules 901–903 |
| ☑ | If the evidence is a writing, recording, or photograph, it is the "best evidence." | Rules 1001–1004 |

# INDEX